Heartfelt
Leadership

"Discover why heartfelt leadership, at every level and in each person, must begin now to make a positive difference in our world."

— COLONEL DEBRA M. LEWIS (US ARMY, RETIRED)
Founder of Mentally Tough Women

"*Heartfelt Leadership* is illuminating. It's shining a big spotlight on something people are fearful to discuss: Do I love the work I do? Is it with purpose and meaning? Do I love the people with whom I work? Do I care so much about them I'm willing to invest in them? I will tell you, for those of us who are there, it feels good. It really does. It's purposeful and meaningful."

—BRITT BERRETT
Program Director of Healthcare Management
Naveen Jindal School of Management at the Univerity of Texas at Dallas

"Deb and Dr. Mark take us through the question of why leaders choose to inject love into a business. Is it innate? Or is it a calculated business decision? The stories from the interviews show us how many of these leaders may follow their heart, but they lead with their soul."

—TIM HINDES
CEO, Stay Metrics

"Society does not advance in a linear way. Rather, it oscillates. Right now, hard edges are all around us. Leadership has taken up once again the bitter skills of using fear to generate allegiance. Separation, loathing, blaming of the other, polarization and hatred abound. But humans ultimately do turn to the light, and we find our better angels. In society and in our workplaces, heartfelt empathy, shared goals, common values and dreams will reassert themselves because over millennia, they always have.

In any corporation or charity, it is possible to use fear in the short-term to propel the team forward. Those five floors of slaves who rowed the freighters across the Mediterranean thousands of years ago, did so under the overseer's whip. But such propulsion is temporary and begrudging. In a free society, people cannot wait to leave.

Great executives do it differently and better, by exerting servant leadership in any organization, by inspiring those working there to grasp the goals and the vision, and to make them their very own. Shared vision and passion is much more achievable. Enduring success is a team sport.

This is one of the strongest books on leadership I have ever read."

—PETER SAMUELSON
Producer of 26 films and founder of five charities that have raised over one billion dollars to serve seriously ill children, foster youth and the homeless

"Relief describes my feeling, knowing now that I'm not alone in my questions and career concerns, relief that I can try new things, and relief that a solution is possible. Thanks to Deb Boelkes and Dr. Mark Goulston for showing us how to create an environment of heartfelt trust and a thirst for self-improvement. Love the stories in the book—so interesting how Deb and Dr. Mark share their voices —it's almost like a dance, flowing back and forth."

—KAREN FRANKENBERG
Chief Financial Officer, Talley, Inc.

"An intriguing book with real life stories, scenarios, and interactions that feel all too familiar, albeit positive or negative. I'd encourage one's extended leadership team to read it as a team so the words come to life, become actionable, and yield shared accountability.

On a few occasions while I was a CEO, I was told that I shouldn't lead from my heart. After reading and considering the words of wisdom in this book, I now recognize that it's not only acceptable to do so, but with refinement can be a positive leadership trait.

Given that interactions and conversations are the backbone of leadership, helping differentiate it from management, the practical stories and challenges in this book will inspire the reader to be better at both, whether in a personal or professional setting.

With *Heartfelt Leadership: How to Capture the Top Spot and Keep on Soaring*, Deb and Dr. Mark truly bring decades of research, real life stories, and courageous examples to stir the reader to action. By opening up as a heartfelt leader, those who embrace the ideas in these pages will attract, retain and motivate their team members to achieve more and be loyal."

—CARYN SIEBERT, JD
Vice President—Carrier Practice, Gallagher Bassett

"The message, the passion, and the commitment Deb and Dr. Mark both have for creating more heartfelt leaders is so appreciated and needed. Thank you for doing the work you both are doing to make the kind of difference that will change our world … coming from our hearts. Now it will become the norm rather than the exception."

—SUSAN INOUYE
Executive Coach, SSI Executive Coaching Solutions

"There are leaders and there are heartfelt leaders. Yes, there is a difference. The result of being a heartfelt leader genuinely fashions a respect and following from others. People know and respond willingly when you act and speak from the heart, not from your position.

Heartfelt Leadership will give you the tools and knowledge to modify your leadership presence. Go from a person who people follow because they have to, to one they want to follow. Deb and Dr. Mark's Heartfelt Leadership group on LinkedIn gave me this knowledge, which in turn brought my leadership to the highest level. I will always be thankful for this."

—DARRELL JANSSEN
Multicultural Engineering Projects Manager

Heartfelt
Leadership

How to
Capture the
Top Spot
and
Keep on
Soaring

Deb Boelkes
with Foreword and Soundbites by
Mark Goulston, M.D.

BUSINESS WORLD RISING, LLC
JACKSONVILLE, FLORIDA

Heartfelt Leadership
How to Capture the Top Spot and Keep on Soaring
© 2020 by Deb Boelkes. All rights reserved.

Book Consultant: Judith Briles, The Book Shepherd
Editor: Barb Wilson, EditPartner.com
Cover and Interior Design: Rebecca Finkel, F+P Graphic Design
Photography of Deb Boelkes: Page Teahan

Library of Congress Control Number: 2020901820
ISBN trade paper: 978-1-7340761-3-4
ISBN eBook: 978-1-7340761-4-1
ISBN audio book: 978-1-7340761-5-8

Business | Leadership | Management

First Edition
Printed in the USA

To the ultimate role models,

Bob and Nancy

Contents

Foreword

Heartfelt Leadership ... say the phrase s-l-o-w-l-y three times with deep breaths in between each time you say it.

When I do that exercise, the first time I say *heartfelt leadership,* I think how much the world needs to do something to stop *heartless* leadership. Okay ... exhale, Mark.

The second time I say those words, I feel what it would be like to work for a heartfelt leader (think of John Wooden and if you're too young to know who he was, look him up). Exhale again, Mark. Ahhh, I'd feel motivated, I'd feel inspired, I'd feel committed, I'd feel dedicated, I'd feel loyal and most of all ... I'd feel safe.

The third time I say those words, I inhale deeply and then exhale. And then I think this is too important not to make it happen.

Heartfelt leadership is not soft woo-woo kumbaya leadership. It is strong and committed leadership that can make the tough decisions, yet be compassionate and caring when it's needed.

What you have in front of you is an inspirational guide with amazingly uplifting, hopeful, and helpful stories that will help you make it happen.

There is no one better to write this than Deb Boelkes, my beloved (and sorely missed, since we live on opposite coasts) cofounder of our Heartfelt Leadership project. In my opinion, she exemplifies this leadership. In addition to great stories, you will hear about the people that Deb and I met in our mission to identify, celebrate, and inspire people to become heartfelt leaders—those who dare to care about their companies and communities.

You'll hear stories from Deb's career. Some of the stories I most admire demonstrate her track record of finding an alternate/next position for those she ever had to let go, and how she helped them land on their feet. If that isn't someone who dares to care, I don't know what is.

Sit back, read, be inspired, and take those three breaths every time you pick up the book because if you do, you will be as committed to bringing heartfelt leadership to the world as we are.

Thank you for daring to care enough to buy this book and join our mission.

—MARK GOULSTON, M.D.
*Talking to Crazy: How to Deal with the Irrational
and Impossible People in Your Life*

ONE

Passion and Engagement

Why don't we stand up to people who,
day after day, sap our enthusiasm and vitality?
—MARK GOULSTON, M.D.
Author, *Get out of Your Own Way at Work ...*
and Help Others Do the Same

What's your typical reaction when you see a phone call from your boss ring in? Do you smile with joyous expectation?

Do you grumble to yourself: "Oh no … what now?"

Or do you reluctantly take the call, wishing you could get away with letting it forward to voicemail … permanently.

If you are a manager, have you noticed how your team members tend to respond when you suddenly appear? Do they smile warmly and eagerly greet you like a long-lost friend? Or do they pretend not to see you and busily hunker down, intently focused on their computer screen or smartphone?

As the manager, do you even notice how your team members react when you walk past? Are you so keenly focused on your task at hand that the only person you see is the one you're looking for to address some important issue? Is *making the numbers* the #1 priority of your eight-to-five modus operandi?

While I'm not proud to admit it, I know I've been guilty of the numbers-making game myself more than once. Throughout my career, I routinely found my teams and I achieved far better results and sustained far higher morale when the personal priorities of each person on the team aligned with the goals of the organization.

For the most part, my personal passions lie in inspiring the passions of others. Doing so inspires me. It feeds my soul. Unfortunately, I only occasionally reported to leaders who displayed any such passion themselves, but I never let that stop me from demonstrating what I believed was the best way to lead.

I recall a few occasions when my most important mission for the good of the organization was to protect my team from an infuriating or disengaging up-line manager. Together, my teams and I created our own sense of family, camaraderie, and fervency for our mission, regardless of upper management.

Why does there seem to be so few heartfelt leaders?

Along the way, I acquired a reputation as an engaging and passionate, heartfelt leader who inspired teams. As a result, we rarely had trouble filling vacancies in our organization. Exceeding our numbers was simply a byproduct of all the fun things we enjoyed accomplishing together.

How many managers have you reported to—or how many peers have you worked with—who energized and inspired you? Have you ever had a manager who caused you to believe, in your role, you could accomplish something significant and important *to you*? If you are like most people, your answer is probably "no."

Given the number of topflight business schools in the world and the number of best-selling leadership books published in the last half century, why does there seem to be so few heartfelt leaders? You would think business schools and military academies would be cranking out thousands of outstanding heartfelt leaders, the kind for whom we would all do anything.

If such leaders were as prolific as one could expect, millions of employees and their leaders would be achieving successes beyond our wildest imaginations every day, in every aspect of society.

Why, then, is this not so?

A few years back, I was leading worldwide business operations for a Fortune 500 technology company. I was invited to participate as one of five executives on a panel discussion at a local technology association event. The discussion topic was "Passion and Engagement."

The other panelists were some fairly well-known C-level executives from the local area. One was the cofounder and chief executive officer (CEO) of a privately held multistate restaurant chain. Another was vice president of human resources (HR) for a large financial services company, and so on. I was just as interested in hearing what they had to say as I was anticipating sharing my leadership philosophies.

The panel discussion began with each of us being asked the same questions. Eventually the moderator allowed the audience to ask individually targeted questions. It was interesting to hear how distinctly different the answers were from each panelist.

About three-quarters of the way through the event, one gentleman from the audience stated to the restaurant chain CEO and the VP of HR: "You two clearly lead from your heads, by the numbers. I think we can all relate to that. But you …" he said, now pointing to me, "… you lead from your *heart*, and we all know there is no room for that in business."

Really?

Perhaps for the first time in my life, I was speechless.

Mind you, this was supposed to be an executive level discussion on "Passion and Engagement." Did this guy really think it was possible to create a culture of passion, engagement, and stellar achievement "by the numbers," without appealing to people's hearts … without appealing to each individual's personal priorities?

> Businesses would be far more successful if there were more leaders who used their heads to touch hearts. It's not an either/or proposition.

This guy obviously didn't know me. But anyone who ever had known me in the business world would most likely describe me as a business strategist who also happens to be pretty passionate about what I do. Few who know me would ever refer to me as someone who purely leads from the heart. Virtually no one who knows me would ever call me emotional—not even my husband.

Yet, as someone who rose to leadership from the male-dominated high tech industry sales ranks, I know only too well people buy into ideas based on emotion ... what they feel in their heart. Then they find a way to cost justify their decision and make the numbers work. A good sales person plays to the client's heart ... as do the best leaders.

That's how outstanding results are achieved. You get to people through their heart. You inspire them. Essentially, when you help people achieve what they care about most, when you engage their emotions, when their personal priorities are aligned with your business objectives, *that's* when you will achieve stellar results. It's not about you manipulating the numbers. The numbers get made as a result of reaching hearts.

This guy clearly didn't get it.

Could it be *most leaders* don't get it? Could it be *most people* in the business world don't get it?

Not only *is* there room in business, the world would be a better place —and businesses would be far more successful—if more leaders used their heads to touch hearts. It's not an either/or proposition.

Shortly after this panel discussion episode, I met Dr. Mark Goulston for the first time at a women's leadership conference where he was the keynote speaker. Perhaps it was the way I gushed over him when I asked him to personally autograph my well-worn, yellow highlighted, dog-eared hardback copy of his book *Just Listen.* My enthusiasm convinced him to suggest we should have a business lunch together soon.

When we eventually did meet for lunch a few weeks later, I shared my "Passion and Engagement" panel discussion story with him. Upon hearing my story, Dr. Mark immediately did a quick Google search on his smartphone. To our surprise, we found these two words—*Heartfelt* and *Leadership*—had never been put together to that point as a web domain, a book title, a training program, or an online community.

After a bit more conversation, we compared notes about my thirty-plus years of leadership experience in Fortune 500 high tech companies and our respective experience coaching and mentoring hundreds of managers and executives across numerous industries. We quickly concluded heartfelt leadership—leadership that inspires people to act from desire, plays to their heart, instills passionate engagement, and results in success—was something the world desperately needed. We instantly agreed to collaborate and write a book on the subject.

Upon further investigation we found many people, from all over the world, intrinsically knew what the term *heartfelt leadership* meant. Many eagerly pointed out to us someone they believed to be a heartfelt leader, but sadly, we found very few who claimed to report to one at work. Not surprisingly, some people actually expressed fear of being viewed as one, lest they be ridiculed or scoffed at, just as I had been during the panel discussion.

So, Dr. Mark and I set out on a five year journey looking for heartfelt leaders. We spent months ferreting out those all too rare organizations where employees love to go to work each day and where customers, when asked, willingly and eagerly praised the organization's products, services, and customer care practices.

It wasn't necessarily easy to find these organizations. In a few cases, exuberant employees proactively recommended we interview their truly beloved and inspiring leader. When our interviews confirmed their leader was indeed a Heartfelt Leader, we invariably also discovered the organization had industry-leading performance.

In other cases, we sought out those few organizations that received "Best Place to Work" awards multiple years in a row *and* consistently ranked at the top of their industries in terms of financial performance and customer satisfaction. Lo and behold, in almost every such case, we found a heartfelt leader at the helm.

We then went on to conduct face-to-face interviews with dozens of heartfelt leadership nominees, as identified by their staffs, customers, and/or industry peers, from a variety of business sectors across America. Both on and off camera, we asked these designated heartfelt leaders to share their personal stories, their business philosophies, and the leadership strategies that enabled their organizations to become the top performers in their respective lines of work.

In the initial phase of this journey, we invited our first few identified heartfelt leaders from the southern California area to join us in onstage interviews at the world's first Heartfelt Leadership symposium. The audience response following the event was overwhelmingly positive. The entire audience *and* the speaker lineup were hungry and anxious to learn more.

Yet, one thing troubled us. We were confounded by the fact over 95% of the conference attendees were women business leaders, even though a third of the heartfelt leaders we interviewed on stage were men. Why did so few men attend this event?

We asked the men who were there that day whether they believed men, in general, were afraid to be viewed as heartfelt leaders lest they be ridiculed. Certainly the men who participated in the onstage interviews at this first Heartfelt Leadership symposium were quite comfortable in their own skins. In fact, these men stated emphatically the world needed MORE heartfelt leaders.

Based on their experience, these men claimed it was the strongest, most self-confident men who were revered as heartfelt leaders and who achieved the greatest success, both in business and in life.

At that first Heartfelt Leadership symposium, we concluded the biggest challenges were these:

- Too few role model heartfelt leaders
- No training programs to teach people to be heartfelt leaders
- No books on the subject for people to read on their own, in their own time.

The purpose of this book and my previous book, *The WOW Factor Workplace: How to Create a "Best Place to Work" Culture*, is to address these challenges.

Initially, we wondered if we would find heartfelt leaders to have similar backgrounds. We wondered if they would be more prolific in certain-sized companies or specific industries. Interestingly, we found NO correlation in gender, childhood upbringing, parental wealth, college degree, company size, or industry.

Heartfelt leaders are, for now, a rare breed.

In fact, we eventually concluded heartfelt leaders come from all walks of life. They are as likely to have had bad role models as good ones in business and in life. We discovered each one we met with had his/her own unique personal style. They can be found in just about any industry, in any size company, and at any level on the organization chart. The one common trait they all seemed to share was the earlier in life they became heartfelt leaders, the faster they and their organizations achieved insane WOW factor success.

Within these pages, you will hear from some truly exceptional award-winning bosses who have been consistently praised by their teams as the epitome of *best-ever bosses*. You will hear in their own words how they became the kind of leaders they evolved into.

By sharing some of the most inspiring executive interviews we conducted during our five-year research process, we hope you will gain the insights and confidence needed to be a heartfelt leader yourself … and therefore become more successful as you take your organization—wherever you are on the corporate ladder, in whatever industry you are in—to new heights.

One thing is certain. Heartfelt leaders are, for now, a rare breed. It is our hope, by reading this book and by taking each of these personal stories to heart, you will help us change that. By using the insights in this book as the foundation for a new kind of leadership development, we hope to produce more role model heartfelt leaders, one leader at a time, beginning with you.

Dr. Mark and I are focused on the outcomes of heartfelt leadership and we believe you are, too. Take this book as inspiration and be flexible in your application of the principles presented here. There are certainly no one-size-fits-all answers or tactics for effectively leading individual people or dealing with specific situations. Effective, inspirational, results-oriented leadership is all about adapting your style and manner of communication with each person and each situation you face.

Don't be surprised to find, in the long run, you may have to keep adapting what you do. The world around us evolves quickly, and if you are successful in transforming yourself into a heartfelt leader, your team members and the level of results you deliver together will evolve quickly, too. You can certainly use these same guiding principles to address new and bigger challenges, yet you will likely need to apply them differently. Simply use your head to touch hearts. That's what the most outstanding leaders do.

We hope the insights we provide in this book will make that possible.

Now, read on and enjoy your journey to heartfelt leadership.

Soundbite FROM DR. MARK

My last living mentor, Warren Bennis, died in 2014. Warren was not just admired and respected; he was beloved. I think it was because within two minutes of meeting him, you got this feeling you could trust him to never hurt you. That's a rare quality in this world and I remember him appearing pleased to be characterized that way.

I first met Warren in 2005 when I was attending one of his classes at USC in a course entitled *The Art and Adventure of Leadership* he co-led with then-college president, Steven Sample. That was the beginning of my intellectual and emotional love affair with him.

On one occasion I said to him, "Warren, I have a confession to make. I've been using you." I told him, "Every time I'm with you I realize and appreciate not only how much you mean to me but I feel you are healing feelings of unworthiness, uninterestingness, and less-than-ness in me. When I feel that healing, I cry with relief at feeling more whole."

Warren then looked at me, put his hand on his chin and delivered his verdict: "That's not a bad way to *use* me, Mark."

After I returned to my office, I emailed Warren: "I know the world is much better for your having been in it. I know that because I am much better for your being in my life."

Years ago, I attended a tribute to Warren at USC. Many wonderful and loving things were said about him by close long-time friends, including the late Sidney Harmon and Betsy Myers, a mentee and protégé of Warren, and a renowned leadership expert herself. At the conclusion of the comments, Warren went to the podium. In his charming, ironic, and playful manner, he said: "One of the great things about hearing so many nice things about you is it gives you something to live up to."

I think it's safe to say Warren has lived up to any and everything people have ever said about him.

I owe Warren a thank you for causing me and so many others to feel interesting and for everything he did to make the world a better place.

We will carry on his mission to study, identify, and develop the best leaders possible.

ACTION STEPS

1 Next time you happen to walk past your team members in your place of business, take note of how they react when you come near. Do they seek you out and react to you with enthusiasm, or do they tend to ignore your presence?

2 Review the mission, vision and business objectives for your organization. Are your personal goals, passions, and priorities in alignment with your organization's mission, vision, and objectives? In your current role, do you honestly believe you can accomplish significant things that are important to you? If not, why not?

3 If you manage others, are you aware of the personal passions, priorities, and goals of those on your team? Have you made it a priority to ensure the natural talents and personal objectives of each member of your team are aligned with the mission, vision, and goals of your organization? If not, why not?

TWO

Go Back
to the Basics

I think it's very simple.
We learn these basics as we are raised as children.
—PAUL SPIEGELMAN
Cofounder of the Small Giants Community

For the first eighty-five years of the twentieth century, the majority of workers in corporate America stayed with the same firm throughout their entire careers. After my dad got out of the Army, he worked for one company his entire career … and he really seemed to love his job.

There was laughter at our dinner table nearly every night as he would tell stories about his workday. He explained with great zeal how he achieved his lofty position in the company. I especially loved hearing, over and over, about the times when he was a young sales rep at IBM, wearing his first business suit, always with a white shirt, a conservative striped tie and wingtip shoes, selling office products like the famed IBM Selectric typewriter.

You could see the sparkle in his eyes as he would reminisce how, day by day, he learned the importance of being friendly and kind to everyone at work. He talked about being especially nice to the secretaries at his customers' offices, the ones who used typewriters. He spoke with pride about how IBM's latest model typewriters could help make a secretary's job easier. I'm sure those secretaries felt pretty special whenever he showed up.

It was easy for me to see how Dad became so successful; why his customers and staffs loved him; how the organizations he led over the years became so profitable; and why he seemed to love every minute of his career. He touched the hearts of those around him and his results seemed nothing short of amazing.

He set the leadership bar for me and instilled in me a desire to become a happy and successful business leader just like him. Although he probably never heard the term back then, from my point of view, he was a heartfelt leader. Together, he and my mom served as my heartfelt leadership role models. From them I learned the importance of helping others to become happy and successful, too.

They enthusiastically loved their jobs, they felt lucky to work where they did, and they never wanted to work anywhere else.

As Dr. Mark and I conducted our heartfelt leadership research, we uncovered a rare breed of leaders who were eagerly referred to us by their staffs as "the best boss I ever had." These leaders were found in a range of industries and occupations scattered across the country, yet they all seemed to share a common leadership philosophy about the importance of relationships and inspiring others.

Not surprisingly, the referring staff members all seemed to have something in common, too: they enthusiastically loved their jobs, they felt lucky to work where they did, and they never wanted to work anywhere else.

Moreover, these businesses all seemed to have reputations for delighting their customers. Their customers referred to these businesses as their favorite suppliers, often in industries otherwise plagued with high turnover and cost-cutting measures that only served to undermine customer satisfaction. As a result, the businesses referred to us stood head and shoulders above the rest in terms of financial performance. They were indeed WOW factor workplaces.

While interviewing these revered leaders, we asked each of them the same opening question:

"When, where, and from whom did you learn the values that have gotten you where you are today?"

While their answers varied greatly, several shared loving reflections of lessons they learned as children "working" alongside their dads.

One heartfelt leader we interviewed was Howard Behar, now retired from his role as president of Starbucks Coffee, and author of the book, *It's Not About the Coffee: Lessons on Putting People First from a Life at Starbucks.* He is well-known for his sense of customers as people, his concern for their needs, and his experience of being a part of people's dreams for their lives.

Howard joined Starbucks in 1989 when the company had just begun to venture outside the Pacific Northwest region. Initially serving as vice president of sales and operations, he grew the retail business from 28 stores to more than 400 by the time he was named president of Starbucks Coffee International in 1995. Under Howard's leadership, Starbucks opened its first location in Tokyo in 1996. Following this historic opening, over the next three years he introduced the Starbucks brand across Asia and the United Kingdom. After a two-year hiatus, he returned to Starbucks as president of Starbucks North America until his retirement in January 2003. He served as a director of the company from 1996 to 2008.

Howard shared this story of how his dad cared for people:

> I think it's like many things in life. We learn a lot growing up. Certainly, this idea about caring about people came early for me. My father was an immigrant to Seattle in the early 1900s. He came without being able to speak the language. He worked in a public market, saved his nickels and dimes, and ended up having a small mom-and-pop grocery store.
>
> I remember growing up as a kid. I would work in the grocery store as a five, six, or seven-year-old kid. We wouldn't call it work, but I was in the grocery store. Occasionally, my father would tell me to go get something out of the back. "Howard, go get some bananas," or "Howard, go get some potatoes," or something. It was usually for a customer who was there. He would take whatever I gave him and he would put it in the bag.
>
> I was about eight or nine years old when I said to him, "Dad, I think you forgot to ring that up on the cash register," because I didn't see him push the buttons.

After the customer had left, he said to me, "Well, let me tell you why I do that. You see, all these people who come into our store, they're all our neighbors. They're not just customers. They are human beings. We supply them the food they need to subsist on. Sometimes people can't afford to buy all the things they need. Every once in a while, when I see they haven't picked up something I know they'd really like to have, I always think I need to help them out. So that's what I do. When I ask you to go get some strawberries and I put them in the bag and I don't ring them up, it's just my way of saying, 'I care about you. You're more important to me than just being a customer. You're a human being and you're a friend.'"

I think that started the idea we all have some level of responsibility for our friends, for our neighbors. In some way, it had to be more than the people who came through that grocery store door just being a customer. They were human beings. It wasn't about the money they had in their pockets. It was about who they were.

We had charge accounts. They would charge and sometimes people couldn't pay. My dad survived poverty as a child. He survived the depression in the United States. He just had a strong set of values about what it meant to be of service to other human beings. No question, I was proud of that. And I was proud because everybody loved my dad. Al Behar's Grocery. The neighbors loved him.

I used to go deliver groceries around the neighborhood, to people who would call in an order. They'd always put their arm around me and hug me and say, "We love your dad." I knew it was because of how he treated them. They knew he cared about them. No question, I was proud of that fact. I was proud of my dad. It was a little tiny grocery store. It wasn't like it was some big Safeway or something like that. But I was proud we were part of that neighborhood. Everyone knew and loved him. Our community celebrated him. Looking back, that was part of my life, part of an immigrant's life.

> **There was something like a glue that bound us together, this caring about each other.**

My mother's family had all come over. She was part of eleven children. They were always taking care of each other. That's all I saw. When one was sick, all the rest of them would bring food. Our friends were my aunts and uncles and cousins. We would go to their houses for dinner. They would come to our house for dinner. There was always laughter and joy and sometimes arguments about things.

But there was something deeper than just that. There was something like a glue that bound us together, this caring about each other that just kind of transferred to me. I didn't really understand it, exactly. I didn't say, "Well, gee, that's a value: caring. That's the value of caring." I didn't interpret it that way until I got older. But I was this guy who liked doing things for others. I felt better about myself when I did. I didn't really understand all that.

Then as I got older, into my mid-to-late twenties, I started to think about that and what all those things meant. I started to search, to try to figure out who I was. How did all of these things play? It came out of a time of pain for me, a time of personal growth. But it informed how I wanted to live my life. As I became more conscious about it, I became more competent as well. It really drove me to think about serving other people.

I think it's just been part of my life. But I'm not just this altruistic guy who never thinks about his own needs. I do. But I find my own needs get met when I'm serving others.

Another heartfelt leader we interviewed was Tim Hindes, former truck driver and dispatcher, now CEO of Stay Metrics, a provider of driver retention tools. Tim transitioned to management early in his trucking career and eventually became a highly successful serial entrepreneur. He was perhaps most widely known because of his passion for creating cultures that put the wants and needs of employees at the forefront.

In creating Stay Metrics, Tim and his business partner teamed up with top researchers in behavioral psychology, management, and organizational culture to create a rewards-and-recognition platform that promotes a better culture and work experience for drivers in the trucking industry. Tim is proud to serve as the real-life poster child of Stay Metrics' core values: passionately put people first; never quit getting better; and do the right thing. Tim shared this story of his dad:

My father was a wonderful man. He was from Harvard, Michigan. When I was a kid, he actually taught us business.

He was a salesman. His customers were small arts-and-crafts supply stores. He would actually go into these stores and write the orders. As a kid (I'm the youngest of eight), we could go to work with him. We'd have to put a shirt and tie on, but we got to have lunch and we got to spend the day with Dad.

As a ten-year-old kid, I would see him go into the stores.

"Hello, Margaret!"

"Hello, Jack!" they would greet each other.

These weren't just customers of his. They were friends.

He was really, truly friends with these people. He would go start their coffee pot.

"How's Ray doing, healthwise?"

He was really, truly concerned. These weren't just customers of his. They were friends.

As a ten-year-old kid it occurred to me, from a business perspective, while they were at the counter he would just be going up and down the aisles writing the orders. He'd be checking his customer's inventory and noting any supplies that were running low. Then he'd write up an order ticket. Ultimately, he'd go to the counter and his customer would just trust him and sign the order.

At about twelve years old, I remember being in the car with him. I said, "You know, I just figured something out." He said, "What's that?"

"They buy whatever you tell them to buy."

"Yeah, but with that comes a great deal of pressure."

"What do you mean?"

"You know when we go to the counter and they have something at the counter, and they say, 'Jack. This didn't work.'"

"Yeah."

"Then I'd tell you to take it to the car and I told my customer I'd credit the account."

"Yeah."

"I sold them something that didn't work for their store. So whatever I put on their order, I have to make sure it works for my customer."

After he taught me that, I asked him another thing. "You are actually supposed to turn your orders in on Monday and you never do. You're late."

"You're right. That's part of the problem I have. I don't want to turn that order in sometimes because I'm afraid it's not going to be the right order."

So, I really took that early on as, "Don't sell somebody something, whether they are a customer or an employee, that is not the right product for that person."

Yet another heartfelt leader we interviewed was Paul Spiegelman, founder of BerylHealth and the Beryl Institute, and cofounder of the Small Giants Community, an organization that brings values-based leaders together. These days Paul focuses on the Small Giants Community.

While Paul was CEO of BerylHealth, he led a unique, people-centric culture for a company that won nine *Best Place to Work* awards, including the #2 *Best Medium-Sized Company to Work for in America.* Paul was also honored with the Ernst & Young *2010 Entrepreneur of the Year* award.

Paul told us this story of his dad:

> My dad taught me a lesson. He said, "Always be nice. Never burn a bridge." I'll never forget that.
>
> The best story I can tell you is, I would be with my dad in some mall and somebody would come by who my dad hadn't seen for thirty years. Before my dad was a lawyer, he was a banker, a loan officer for a bank in Los Angeles for many years. He built relationships. I would run into people with him, and I could tell he was great at building relationships. And he never forgot a face.

It's not about the product or the service we have. It's about getting people to like us, building relationships, earning trust.

> More than once, the person he had just run into would pull me aside and say, "You know what? Your dad is one of the nicest people I've ever met." I thought, "I want people to say that about me one day." If people could say that about me, then I would be successful in life.
>
> I think it's very simple. We learn these basics while we are raised as children. If we take the good of that and grow our own lives, then good things are going to happen. I would say

most of my life, the good things and the bad things that have happened in my life have not been deliberate or planned. I think I've let life come to me.

That's the one thing I set out to do: Be nice to people ... not burn a bridge.

I've learned, even though I am an introvert, how to build relationships and how to get people to like me. I realized that's what business is about. It's not about the product or the service we have. It's about getting people to like us, building relationships, earning trust. Then you can do whatever you want to do. That is the basis of my life: trying to build relationships with people.

Now, teaching my children, the first thing I ask them is, every time they have an interaction with a teacher or someone else, "Were they nice?" I'm trying to build the same sort of values into them.

Not all the retrospective values stories we heard from best-ever bosses were of fathers working in consumer-oriented industries. One such story was told by military best-ever boss Colonel Debra M. Lewis (US Army, Retired). A West Point graduate in the first class to include women, Colonel Deb is a battle-tested leader whose subordinates in Iraq lovingly referred to her as a caring leader who worked tirelessly to help them succeed.

Colonel Deb shared this story about her father, Lieutenant General Bennett L. Lewis (US Army, Retired):

He was in the military longer than I was: over 40 years in uniform and served during three major conflicts: World War II, Korea, and Vietnam. He retired as a very senior officer. I'm so proud of all he accomplished. I will tell you, though, to rise to the top he was very fortunate to have some mentors who helped him along the way and a supportive spouse, my mom. Some of the things he did were neither popular nor easy.

Sometimes he had to shake things up. In one situation, government-contracted workers were being mistreated. He would go in, oftentimes incognito, and talk to everyone to get a feel for what was really happening. He'd find out people were not getting paid or they were not getting the guidance to be successful in their job. He'd do whatever needed to happen. Sometimes when my dad started digging around, there would be negative consequences for anyone not taking care of the people, or the task, or blow-back from the people causing the problems because he wouldn't let things go until they were fixed.

He wanted to do what was right, not thinking about the repercussions that might impact him.

I think he demonstrated he always cared about what people were doing. He wanted to do what was right, not thinking about the repercussions that might impact him. He was fortunate to stay so long in service. His people respected him. They wanted to do so much for him and the projects were exciting and needed.

I had a very clear example of someone who really led with a caring heart, a heart for our country, wanting to do what was right by our country. That patriotic flavor certainly was instilled in me very early on.

Now back to my own story. Because my father was so successful and so happy with his own life, both at work and at home, I wanted to follow in his footsteps. My goal upon graduating from MBA school was to become a senior executive for a major corporation like IBM and eventually retire from there after thirty years or so.

Back in those days, large companies were loyal to employees and in return, employees were loyal to the company. I remember Mom telling us how Dad's company, IBM, so cared about its people, even during the Great Depression, they did not lay off their employees. Instead, everyone shared in pay reductions. At least everyone kept their jobs at a time when unemployment across the US rose to 25%.

Back in the day, there was a real focus by the company leadership on camaraderie and keeping spirits high. IBM even had its own employee song book. *Songs of The IBM* was originally published in 1927 on the request of company founder, Thomas J. Watson, Senior. For many

> **To be successful, you have to have your heart in your business, and your business in your heart.**
> —Thomas J. Watson, Sr.

years, new employees in training would start their days in class learning the company songs. How about that for inspiration?

Dad started his sales training as a new employee in the mid-1950s. As part of their orientation training, the young sales recruits had to memorize the company song, *Ever Onward*. To ensure they learned it, first thing each morning the instructor would randomly call upon one of the trainees. They had to stand up and sing the company song, a cappella, in front of the entire class.

Can you imagine singing in front of your new workmates?

I suppose it was not unlike learning your college alma mater as an incoming freshman, except this was the corporate world and these were adults singing about a company to which they would dedicate their entire working lives. They were dedicated to and dependent upon each other for their livelihoods. IBM had a vision and a mission and everyone lived the company's values. These guys and gals were heartfelt. They really cared about the company and for each other.

To this day, Dad says he can still remember attending his first 100% Club, a special annual award event to honor and recognize those sales reps and company leaders who attained their sales quotas for the year. At the beginning of these events all the attendees stood up and sang the company song together … with heartfelt gusto.

As Dad would tell it, when the founder of IBM, Thomas J. Watson, Sr. entered the room, "Everyone stood at attention. It was as though he was the President of the United States. We revered him. We were fervent. Those were the days!"

The opening passage of the 1937 edition of the IBM song book explains how the gatherings and conventions of IBM expressed the "fine spirit of loyal cooperation and good fellowship in happy songs … for the betterment of business and benefit to mankind."

The IBM song book contained no less than 100 fellowship songs that were sung to the tunes of well-known popular songs of the day. Several of them were dedicated to IBM's beloved founder, like the song entitled *To Thos. J. Watson, IBM Our Inspiration*, sung to the tune of "Columbia, the Gem of the Ocean." Other songs were dedicated to division leaders, customer service managers and even assistant sales managers.

These guys and gals were heartfelt. They really cared about the company and for each other.

Think about it. They certainly weren't going to write songs about people who were in and out of the company at the drop of a hat. If your peers wrote a song about you, wouldn't you feel a dedication and an obligation to live up to the legend? It must have been quite a motivator.

Can you imagine the staff at *any* company today singing songs dedicated to the founder or various employees like that? Maybe we'd all be better off if we did.

Until the mid-1980s, when I eventually joined the company, it was assumed every employee who performed to expectations would spend their entire career there. From the moment you were brought on board you became part of "the IBM family." Everyone was invested in the relationship.

With such a dedicated employee base, the company had good reason to help each team member make the most of his or her individual talents and skills. If the company, over time, realized the greatest value from each employee, it was a good return on its investment.

Managers were given incentives to keep a watchful eye open to identify potential rising stars. Anyone so identified was likely to be put into a management development program and given challenging developmental assignments to test his or her mettle. Those who proved worthy were mentored and guided up the ladder. In return, employees were loyal to the company. Everyone gave it his or her all. No wonder our dad's dinnertime tales about his work were told with such zeal and love.

The IBM of yesteryear was a WOW factor workplace inspired by heartfelt leaders.

Soundbite FROM DR. MARK

Do you practice the Diamond Rule where you "do unto others as someone special has done unto you?"

"Why the "Diamond Rule?" you ask.

Because diamonds are forever.

ACTION STEPS

1 Think of someone from your life who you deeply respected and whose esteem for and belief in you meant so much, the last thing you would ever want to do was be anything less than the great person they believed you to be.

2 Select someone in your organization who you could do unto what that special person did unto you ... then go do it.

THREE

When the Going Gets Tough

*I think people start making decisions
less from the heart because they're so nervous
about survival.*

—COLLEEN BARRETT
President Emeritus, Southwest Airlines

I actually began my professional career not at IBM but at AT&T, back then known as "the phone company." Although I had an offer to go to work for IBM right out of graduate school, I didn't want anyone to think I was riding on someone's coattails—my father's! I needed to prove to myself I could be a successful business leader in my own right somewhere else. Silly girl.

Overachiever, that's what I am. I have always been a highly motivated and ambitious overachiever, throwing all my passion and energy into just about everything I did and do. In high school I was class valedictorian. I graduated top in my class in undergraduate school. I was ranked number one in my class in graduate school. I just assumed I would automatically be selected for the fast track in any major corporation I chose to work for. I assumed there would be rapid promotions, especially for a woman with an MBA. There weren't many of us with such credentials at the time and a number of major corporations had programs aimed at promoting women.

I started my career in the fall of 1982 at Pacific Telephone & Telegraph Company, the largest of the twenty-one wholly AT&T-owned "Baby Bells." I was hired to design customer premise-based telephone systems and private branch exchanges for major corporations and large campus environments. As I had expected, I was sent to a myriad of training to learn the skills required of a telephone systems engineer.

It didn't take long for me to figure out working for the phone company, a regulated monopoly, was not at all what I had envisioned while listening to Dad's dinnertime tales of his WOW factor workplace, IBM. The worn, dingy gray linoleum-floored building where I was first assigned in downtown LA was nothing like the slick, modern, all glass, high rise, AT&T showcase where I was interviewed before graduation. It certainly was not the kind of place I had imagined, where spirited and enthusiastic employees sang company songs. Nor did I find many passionate, high energy salespeople there.

To the contrary, my new boss and many of the other long-timers I was assigned to work with seemed to be retired on the job. No one seemed to have any sense of urgency. It wasn't long before I couldn't wait to be reassigned to another part of the corporation.

Shortly thereafter, a government consent decree mandated the breakup of the Bell System—thank goodness. I was thrilled to have the chance to get out from under the shackles of a regulated monopoly and move into the newly deregulated side of the business.

I was even more excited to learn the new entity, American Bell (subsequently renamed AT&T Information Systems), was to be led by an entirely new regime of senior leaders, many recruited from IBM. I was almost giddy over the prospect of having a chance to work for a new business entity, in a brand new, high rise office tower, that would certainly be a much better reflection of what I had imagined of IBM. I eagerly counted the days to divestiture.

With the launch of American Bell, just as I had expected, I was quickly placed on the fast track. I was sent to leadership development training and given more challenging customer assignments. I jumped at the chance to work with the new technologies under development at Bell Labs. I quickly became the regional expert on the latest leading-edge call center products.

For the first year or two, I played leapfrog up the career ladder with a young male colleague who had also transferred in from Pacific Telephone, another ambitious fast tracker who also jumped ship at the first opportunity. Over the ensuing months, every time one of us would get promoted we'd buy the other lunch at some swanky restaurant to celebrate. We had a good natured competition going to see who would buy the next celebration lunch.

I distinctly recall attending a massive company launch event where all the employees in the region came together to meet the new senior leadership team, the former IBM executives. My fast tracker colleague jokingly said to me, "It's obvious, if we want to make it to the top of this company, we're going to have to go work for IBM first."

A short while later I learned his wife actually did work for IBM. The next thing I knew, he left AT&T and went to work for IBM. Meanwhile, I was routinely getting calls from headhunters, but I never dreamed of really leaving AT&T. I never seriously considered any of the external opportunities for promotion presented to me. I was at AT&T to stay.

Then I started getting calls from my former colleague-turned-IBM-employee, inviting me to lunch with his new IBM manager. "Life is really good at IBM," he'd say as he then jokingly reminded me, "if you want to be an executive at AT&T, you first need to join IBM. Why don't you come to lunch and talk to us about it?"

I would laugh and politely reply, "I'll have lunch with you, and I'll be happy to meet your boss, but that's it."

I loved my job and I loved my staff.   AT&T was good to me and I was loyal to AT&T. I had no interest in ever leaving.

Soon I was promoted to management, leading my first organization, AT&T Information Systems' southwest regional Executive Conference Center. Together with the marketing gurus from headquarters, my team and I hosted executive golf tournaments and pizzazz-y national product launches that garnered big media attention. We also coordinated senior executive-level get-togethers where our regional vice president could build relationships with the top executives of our largest national accounts.

I loved my job and I loved my staff. These professionals truly knew how to work magic. I felt so blessed. If this company had had a song book, I would have written company songs for them.

Then, suddenly, something happened to break the magic spell.

One day my boss called me into his plush, cushy office. He never got up from his desk, just briskly motioned me to sit down. We made small talk for a moment or two, but there was none of his usual congeniality. Something was strange.

What? We're laying all of them off?

He then awkwardly informed me I was getting promoted to the next salary grade. Before I could react, he went on to flatly explain I would still be running the Executive Conference Center, but I would no longer have a staff. That's why I was now getting a raise. None of this made sense to me.

"Is my staff being reassigned?" I asked.

"No. You will be laying them off next Tuesday morning," he said coldly.

"What? We're laying all of them off?" I asked in disbelief.

"Yes, YOU will be laying all of them off," he flatly said.

"What did we do wrong?" I asked in shock.

"Nothing," he replied. "We have hundreds of employees here in the region we need to get rid of. Your team has been targeted because they aren't in sales. But you're safe. We still need you here so we're promoting you."

I was completely stunned and confused. I had heard my dad talk about firing people at IBM who weren't performing up to standards, but I had never heard about laying off entire departments when no one had done anything wrong.

As it turned out, AT&T was the first major American corporation during the 1980s to announce a massive corporate downsizing. More than twenty-seven thousand workers would be off AT&T's payroll by early 1987.

"What am I supposed to say to them?" I asked my boss with trepidation. Even with all the AT&T management training I had received by then, I was never taught how to manage a layoff. The subject never even came up.

"I don't know," my manager said. "I've never laid anyone off before, either. But you have until Tuesday morning to figure it out."

I was floored. I felt as though I had just been told I would be leading my team to the guillotine. That weekend was agonizing for me. What would I say?

After much deliberation, I decided the best approach would be to follow the Golden Rule: Do unto others as you would have them do unto you. I knew whatever I would say had to be authentic, from the heart, and honest. Most importantly, I would have to act with compassion, candor and integrity.

> **People will forget what you said,**
> **people will forget what you did,**
> **but people will never forget**
> **how you made them feel.**
> —MAYA ANGELOU
> Author, poet, singer, and civil rights activist

On Tuesday morning, I asked each member of my team, one at a time, to meet with me in my office. As each one came in, I closed the door, sat down next to him or her, and revealed what was going to happen. After the initial mouth-dropping reaction, I continued. Each was told how much I honored, respected, and admired him or her. I talked about the strengths each of them uniquely brought to the team.

It was one of the most difficult days I had ever had to deal with.

Then I asked, "What is important to you in life and what made you excited about your career?" I listened closely to each response.

Rolling up my listening sleeves, each got my undivided attention. We discussed what they would really love to be doing going forward, wherever that might be. We brainstormed about the type of jobs they would love to have. We reviewed the kind of companies in the local region or elsewhere which might have good opportunities for them to do the things they really wanted to do. I gave them my wholehearted commitment to help them get there.

It was one of the most difficult days I had ever had to deal with up to that point. Yet, by the end of the day, it seemed we were drawn even closer together. Helping each one find his or her next dream job became my top priority for the next few months. At that time, employees were given plenty of notice prior to termination.

Phone calls were made to several of our local clients to inquire about potential job opportunities for each member of my staff. I wrote referral letters; coached and mentored my team members through the interview process; and brainstormed stretch assignments they could take on in the weeks ahead that would give them more experience doing whatever might better position them for the potential opportunities in which they were interested.

After all was said and done, each of them went off to even better, more exciting positions. A couple of them started their own businesses doing almost exactly what they had been doing for AT&T. When they were finally off the AT&T payroll, I even hired some of them back as contractors, paying them even more on a contract basis than they were earning as employees. I had the budget and the work still had to get done; it made sense. Every single one of them came back some time later to thank me for helping them find the path to an even better career.

I will never forget that experience. For better or worse, the skills I developed during that ordeal were skills I would eventually come to rely upon time and again throughout my corporate career. The times, they were a-changing. *Heartfelt leadership did make a difference.*

Goodbye ... Hello ... and Eyes Opening

A shift was stirring within me. My attitude about the company changed dramatically after that. No longer did I desire to spend the rest of my career there. While it never entered my mind that I might one day be the target of such a layoff, I no longer trusted my senior management team.

Not long after that first round of layoffs, I had another phone call from my former colleague, inviting me to lunch once again with his IBM manager. This time, I accepted their invitation. It wasn't long before I stepped away and accepted IBM's offer to join them.

It was about that time that my father retired from IBM. I felt somewhat relieved I might be able to join the company and not be accused of riding on his coattails. Little did I know that the branch manager I would be reporting to had reported to my dad a few times over the years. Looking back, I have no doubt the fact this manager knew my dad played some factor in my hiring.

I jumped into IBM with gusto. Once again, I started working my way up the management ladder, taking advantage of every leadership training opportunity offered me. I took "challenge" developmental roles. It was great fun for a while, but before long, I discovered this IBM was not what I had envisioned of my father's IBM. Gone were the song books. Gone was the fervor and the zeal.

Another thing I was not at all prepared for was being referred to as a "professional hire." Before I joined the company, professional hires were a rarity. Virtually everyone had been hired right out of college or from the military. Hiring into IBM after some years of professional experience

Laws made it far more difficult to terminate underperformers.

in the corporate world was most unusual back then. For years thereafter, whenever I was introduced to IBM customers or internal higher-ups, I was introduced as "Debra, the professional hire." I suppose it was intended to be a special honor, but somehow I never felt like a "real" IBM employee.

Likewise, just as I found at the phone company, the entitlement syndrome had also begun to settle in at IBM. Perhaps some of the zeal had waned once the Watson family founders were no longer running the business. Some managers blamed it on the increasingly progressive state of employment law designed to protect employees. For better or worse, such laws made it far more difficult to terminate underperformers.

As a work-around, some IBM managers instituted a practice of promoting underperformers, just to get them out of their departments. This led to plummeting morale for the remaining, more ambitious team members. I found it shocking the underperformers were rising well beyond their levels of incompetence rather than being let go. Those who were doing exemplary work now had a more difficult time getting ahead because the open slots higher up were instead being filled with what we came to refer to as "empty suits." Those who delivered exemplary results now stayed in place far longer, unfairly penalized instead with the additional workload left behind by the now-promoted empty suits.

Some longtime employees claimed, after the departure of the Watsons from the helm, executives increasingly focused on business metrics to drive results and less on employee and customer development. Gone was the universal drive for excellence. Gone was the overwhelming respect and love for senior management. Gone.

As the employee malaise took hold, creativity, productivity, and customer relationships were severely impacted. Once-loyal IBM customers opened their doors to more aggressive lean-and-mean startups like Microsoft, Apple, and others. The once true "Big Blue" customer loyalty became a thing of the past. IBM profits plummeted and downsizings became common practice. As the once-zealous IBM family culture evaporated, loyalty disappeared, too.

It's interesting to note, of all the companies listed in the Fortune 500 in 1955—the year the first Fortune 500 list was created—only 12% remained on the list fifty years later. Two of them being AT&T and IBM. The technology industry was not the only industry segment impacted by such culture shifts.

The airline industry also underwent a wholesale culture shift. Once regulated air carriers who had been guaranteed a reasonable rate of return now struggled to break even. After the 1950s, airline yields (defined as the average fare paid by a passenger per flight mile) consistently dropped. What had formerly been a luxurious event in the early days of Pan Am ultimately degenerated into a grumble-worthy experience, for the most part.

As airlines continued to reduce leg room and seat width in attempts to get more butts in seats on each flight, overall consumer satisfaction and even flight attendant satisfaction took a nose dive, a dive that for many still continues.

I had the opportunity to speak with heartfelt leader, Colleen Barrett, president emeritus and corporate secretary of Southwest Airlines, about this culture shift phenomenon. Colleen was there back when Herb Kelleher founded the company, originally called Air Southwest. As a high frequency, low fare, point-to-point US-based airline that was established to give everyday people the freedom to fly, Southwest Airlines takes great pride in its excellent customer service qualities to this very day.

Colleen shared this perspective:

> Unfortunately, I think we're going backward versus forward. It really doesn't matter whether we're talking about corporate America, whether we're talking about the United States, whether we're talking about the world, or whether we're talking about politics. It seems to me everything is becoming very programmed. There's nothing from the heart that goes into almost any decision. This is a pet peeve of mine, just to be honest.

The airline industry is so competitive and the economy was so weak for so long, I think people started making decisions less from the heart because they were so nervous about survival.

Yes, we've had challenges. We've had humongous challenges. I actually think at Southwest, what we call the "Warrior Spirit" was actually created by our enemies versus by us being such brilliant leaders when we said, "Okay, we need a warrior spirit." I think it was a matter of survival.

It was those people out there fighting us, keeping us on the ground, and then when we got back in the air, they were convinced they could put us back on the ground. They were so cocky about it. I think our people didn't have to be asked, "Hey, will you go out on your day off and throw flyers around the city of Dallas?" If they didn't, they knew they weren't going to get a paycheck. They were that scared. It created such a bond with people, honestly, if you tried to create it, tried to manipulate it, it wouldn't work, probably. But it was real. It was genuine.

People started making decisions less from the heart because they were so nervous about survival.

I don't know, but I am worried the country is going the other way and most of corporate America is going the other way as well.

Starbucks' Howard Behar shared this personal story about how the leader of one company he worked for early in his career impacted his well-being:

I worked for a company called Grantree Furniture Rental. I had gotten a promotion and one day the chairman/CEO of the company came to me and said, "Howard, we really love you. You have done a great job. You deserved the promotion. *But,* there are some things I think you ought to change about yourself."

Of the things he asked me to change, one went to the core of who I was as a human being: how I process things. I was passionate and emotional back then. I'm still the same now. He didn't think being emotional was good when you wanted to be an executive. He tried to get me to change. It was a very difficult process for me and I couldn't. I became depressed over it. It was the first time I'd ever really suffered any depression I can remember, of any kind.

In my attempt to change, I realized it wasn't me. I could not go there. I could not be what he wanted me to be. The problem was, I didn't know who I was. I was just Happy Howard, Bad Howard. They'd call me "Happy Howie."

When I went through that process at that time, I decided, "I'm not going through this again. If anybody ever again says, 'Howard, we think you ought to be something other than who you are,' I want to at least have a discussion about who I am."

Donald Stamets, general manager for the Flagship Solage, an Auberge Resort located in Calistoga, California, in the heart of Napa Valley, is someone I have personally known for some time to be a heartfelt leader. Knowing his team members lovingly refer to themselves as *#TeamDonald*, I was delighted to interview him for this book. Donald has spent his entire 30+ year career in the hospitality industry, including fifteen years with the Ritz-Carlton Hotel Company, known worldwide for treating guests like royalty.

During our conversation, I asked Donald if he ever had a manager who didn't display the leadership ethos one might expect to find in service-renowned organizations like Auberge Resorts or Ritz-Carlton. Here is what he said:

Well, there was one leader. I can remember like it was yesterday, working for a separate hotel company. Everything he taught me was what NOT to do. I don't think he taught me anything about what TO do in the three years I was with him.

I go back to my initial learnings as a child: "It's only 20% what he does to you. It's 80% how I react to it." I chose to remain positive and to deflect his negativity with my positivity. He knew he could never crack me.

I was his number two. I was really the GM of the property when it was voted the "Best Resort in the Country." His leadership style was toxic. The turnover in that resort was overwhelming because of his leadership style. Then, in the years I was there, the turnover reduced because I then became the filter between him and the rest of the associates. That was the year we won, voted by *Conde Nast:* "The #1 Resort in the Country."

So, I have worked with individuals with whom I don't see eye-to-eye. Again, I treat them with the same respect and dignity as I would treat someone who has and shares the same values I have. I find a way that motivates them. I work with them as individuals, not as a group of people. I just became the filter between him and the rest of the associates in that resort.

Don't ever be afraid to make any decision. Don't ever be afraid of your dreams.

I replied to Donald, "That's a tough position to be in."

Nodding in agreement, he added:

It was. I only lasted three years. He's still there today. He is a brilliant hotelier. He just has a different leadership style than I do and is very successful. I just chose to separate after a while.

Don't ever be afraid to make any decision. Never be afraid to say, "This leader and my style ... I've worked my butt off for this company and I've tried to do everything I possibly can ... life is too short to live in this toxicity."

I was with Ritz-Carlton for fifteen years. I had a great opportunity to work in another brilliant organization. I loved Ritz-Carlton but I made the decision to leave. I've said it before: without risk, there is no reward. So, don't ever be afraid of your dreams.

This is something else I always say to all my leaders and I know my chef repeats it back to me all the time. He says, "My head is always above the clouds, sir."

I say, "That's right. You know why?"

He'll say, "Why?"

I'll say, "Because it's always sunny up there."

If your head is below the clouds, you have rain, storms, wind, and all that other stuff. Keep your head up above the clouds. It's always sunny and beautiful up there. So just keep moving forward.

It's hard to top that, but in closing this chapter, let's go back to Southwest Airlines to hear from role model heartfelt leader, Teresa Laraba. Until her passing on Christmas day in 2015, Teresa was senior vice president of customers for Southwest Airlines. She worked for Southwest throughout her entire adult career.

My mother told me growing up, "No relationship is a waste. Any relationship you walk away from where you learn something, good or bad, you learn something. No relationship is ever a waste." I believe that in any professional business, too ... if you invest in people, there is never a waste.

I can certainly relate to Teresa's lesson-learned and perhaps you can, too. I find when I keep my mind open, I learn something from virtually everyone I interact with.

Believe it or not, I find just about everyone I meet to be amazing, if I just ask the right questions. Sometimes I learn a small thing, perhaps a reinforcement of a belief. Sometimes I learn a WOW thing, or have a great "ah ha!" moment. Occasionally it's something I hope to never experience again. But one thing is for certain: I always learn something from every relationship. As Teresa's mother told her, "No relationship is a waste."

Looking back over the years, it seems I may have learned more "what *not* to do" from a number of managers and executives I have worked with. The important thing is this: in those situations, I always asked myself what I should do differently so *I'm* not that kind of leader. Sometimes my conclusion is simply "not *that*." But at least I learned something.

Soundbite FROM DR. MARK

Many great people I know are or have been people who have done heartfelt things but have not been heartfelt leaders.

I think the difference is many people who do great and generous things benefit others, but also serve their own ambition, personal agendas, and egos. You can tell those people because they rarely do anything anonymously or if they do, they have a way of letting info slip out so people know who they are.

When you do things and take credit for it, or say "we did it" when it's clearer in your tone "you did it," your higher purpose is contaminated by a self-serving, attention-seeking agenda. Now don't get me wrong, it's better for these great projects to be undertaken and someone's name attached to it than to not have the projects done at all.

On the other hand, what's remarkable about heartfelt leaders is they are more about heartfelt *being* than heartfelt *doing*. Their immense heartfelt doing is just a byproduct of their heartfelt being, a byproduct of their innate goodness, kindness, and generosity. Heartfelt leaders are also more likely to do things anonymously. They tend to show great discomfort when they are given too much credit for team results.

ACTION STEPS

1   Think back on your career. Did you ever have a job where you initially loved the company, but your enthusiasm deteriorated over time?

2   List the things you most loved about that company.

3   Determine where your breaking point occurred. Assess which factors had the biggest negative impact on your outlook.

4   Think of the worst job you ever had. Ask yourself these questions:

- How did people treat each other?
- How did people on your team behave, in general?
- What was the overall level of performance?
- Were there goals for the overall organization and/or for your department?
- Did you have your own goals? If so, who defined them?
- How loyal were the employees?
- How loyal were the lower and mid-level managers?
- How loyal were the customers (or clients, patients, patrons, or donors)?

FOUR

Create Genuine Magic

When you get to know her and see how passionate and how personal the mission is for her—to really care for people—it is so genuine; you can't help but be driven by it and admire it.

—TERESA LARABA
Senior Vice President of Customers, Southwest Airlines

It doesn't matter where you are on the organizational chart. Of course, CEOs can make huge impacts by setting the mood from the top down. But you don't have to wait until you become a CEO or even a mid-level manager to make a big impact and inspire those around you to be the best they can be.

As we've seen already, great leaders, heartfelt leaders, can be found at all levels in an organization, in any industry, and in every kind of workplace. Whether you are managing up, down or across an organization, you can ignite the kind of spirit that can bring about extraordinary results inside the company and beyond.

I was born and raised in Southern California. It seemed we went to Disneyland dozens of times when I was young. I could never get enough of "The Happiest Place on Earth." I loved it back then and I still do.

I can remember going there before I was four years old. The drive from our home to Disneyland was probably no more than forty minutes, but it seemed like an eternity driving past all the orange groves that used to be in Orange County. I would get so excited every time it was announced we were going to Disneyland, the Magic Kingdom. I couldn't wait to get there. To this day, I still get excited to go to any Disney park, anywhere in the world.

With more than sixty years in the theme park business, Disney has always known how to deliver a WOW factor experience. Maybe that's why, for years, Disneyland and Walt Disney World have placed ads on TV following the Super Bowl, featuring short, on-the-field interviews with the game's Most Valuable Player. The interviewer would say, for example, "Peyton Manning, you've just won the Super Bowl. What are you going to do next?"

The answer from the one person who had just lived the single most WOW factor experience one might ever imagine was, "I'm going to Disneyland!"

Where else would anyone go after an incomparable experience like winning the Super Bowl, but to the Happiest Place on Earth, the Magic Kingdom? It never disappoints.

Knowing how I feel about Disneyland—or Walt Disney World, or Epcot Center, or you-name-it Disney park—you may not be surprised to learn my first job working for a major corporation was at Disneyland. I loved that job so much I couldn't believe I actually got paid to work there. I honestly would have worked there for free. The pay was just icing on the cake.

Have you ever felt that way about a job?

Mind you, when I worked at Disneyland, I was just a seventeen-year-old high school senior. My position at Disneyland was at the very bottom of the organizational chart. I was a cast member, a "marching card," the ace of clubs with the *Alice in Wonderland* dance unit. Our dance team performed twice each day in the magical Christmas Parade along Disneyland's Main Street during the winter holiday season. To this very day, whenever I go to any Disney venue and hear the song we used to march to over the loud speakers, I still feel that same old thrill and immediately step into that marching card dance routine—at least in my mind. I get that same big, sparkling smile on my face. I'll never forget the exhilarating feeling of performing at Disneyland as long as I live.

Landing any job in the Park was a real achievement.

Being part of the Disneyland Christmas Parade was an amazing experience. From the dancers and the band members to the rest of the cast of Disney characters, every cast member in the parade was an amazing showman. It was an indescribable honor to be part of a team you believed with all your heart was amazing. We all had incredible respect for each other. We were there to make magic happen and that's just what we did. Everyone in the audience seemed to believe we were marching cards, as though we had just stepped through the looking glass from Wonderland.

There was one work rule for all Park cast members that was absolutely non-negotiable: you were ALWAYS to be 100% in costume and in character whenever you were clocked in and visible in any public area of the Park.

I remember being told that our parade director, who I only ever saw out of costume in the Employees-Only section of the Park, played the role of Mickey Mouse in the parade. But since I never actually saw him even partially out of costume back stage, I never really knew if the Parade Director really played Mickey Mouse in the parade or not. Of course, you couldn't tell it from his voice. Mickey always looked and sounded like Mickey. The rest was magic.

Landing any job in the Park was a real achievement. For cast member applicants still in high school or college, one had to have a "B" grade-point average or better in order to be hired; not to mention you had to beat out some extremely talented competition.

Because our marching card dance unit was just a temporary seasonal role, these cast members had a very short timeframe in which to learn and perfect their dance routines. Consequently, Disneyland held a competitive audition to find "the best of the best" of dance drill teams already accustomed to performing together in perfect synchronization.

Our one-day competitive audition was held on a Saturday in a back lot at Disneyland. Every high school dance drill team from across Southern California must have been invited to compete.

The winning team would be hired as a team to perform together for the duration of the winter holiday season.

Our high school drill team initially held our own competition to select the nine best dancers to represent our school at the audition. I was one of the lucky nine. On the day of the audition at Disneyland, dozens of nine-member dance drill teams participated in the audition. There were three elimination rounds. The winning team at the end of round three would be hired. It was intimidating, to say the least.

For the first elimination round, each dance team performed a unique routine they had created on their own in advance of the competition. Each routine was to last a specific number of seconds. The objective of this first elimination round was to show the judges how creative, precise, synchronized and time-sensitive we could be. It was also to demonstrate our showmanship. We were to exude "Disney Magic" from the first step to the last step. The goal was to be the best team at meeting all the performance criteria. Our team was selected to go on to round two.

For the second elimination round, each dance team was provided a never-seen-before dance script. We were given a couple of hours to interpret the script, turn it into a performance, memorize it, practice it for precision, timing, and showmanship, and then perform it in front of the judges during the afternoon. Each team performed the same routine. By the end of round two, our team made it to the top 10, which allowed us to compete in the final round.

For the final round, we performed the original dance routine we had created ourselves in advance of the competition for round one.

We were simply told to "give it all you've got." We did, and we won. The nine of us were hired as a team. Wow!

Now we had to really perform with passion and engagement.

Whatever you do, do it well.
Do it so well that when people see you do it,
they will want to come back and see you do it again,
and they will want to bring others and
show them how well you do what you do.

—WALT DISNEY
American entrepreneur, animator and film producer

The job itself, to some, might have been considered a bit of a pain. We performed seven days a week, twice each day. The first parade performance of the day was in the midafternoon. The second performance of the day was at nine o'clock at night. We were free to go home in between, but we had to report backstage far enough in advance of each performance to dress in costume and makeup.

Mind you, this included Christmas Eve, Christmas Day, New Year's Eve and New Year's Day. As I recall, we were not paid any overtime. Some young people might have complained about that, but to us it was a joy, an honor, and a privilege just to be there. The opportunity to perform in the Park to an audience of nearly a hundred thousand smiling, cheering, enchanted people was compensation enough.

We had to be perfect. No excuses. Ever.

Before we landed the job, none of us had any idea how many people went to Disneyland on Christmas Eve or Christmas Day.

These holidays happened to be, at least back then, the busiest, most crowded days of the year in the Park. Disneyland actually had to close the main gate for some periods of time to keep the Park from exceeding the maximum capacity. For some families, just going to Disneyland was their Christmas gift. We were part of the present. Knowing that made it even more special for us as performers.

Once we had the job, we each gave our personal best every single moment. We competed against ourselves to set new personal best records with each ensuing performance. If any one of us made a wrong move, it impacted all of us, and it certainly impacted our "guests." We all depended on each other. Disneyland depended on us. The audience who had paid so dearly to attend depended on us. If any one of us failed individually, we all failed. We had to work together at peak performance, in perfect unison, every single time. We had to be perfect. No excuses. Ever.

Keep in mind, we were just individual contributors at the bottom of the org chart, yet each one of us mattered. Each of us had to show up for every single performance. Because of our synchronized routines, if any single one of us was ever absent, the entire unit, including the nine band members who marched in synchronization with us, would have been pulled from the show. So, we gave every performance, each and every day, our individual and collective best efforts to deliver a flawless and magical performance.

As a result, each show *was* a magical, WOW factor experience for one and all. As an enterprise, Disney was a magical, WOW factor workplace that ignited the spirits of guests and employees alike. It was certainly a "Best Place to Work" in our opinion. Consequently, Disney garnered a brand loyalty like no other. This, in turn, generated a healthy bottom line for The Walt Disney Company year after year.

Fast forward 40+ years. The Walt Disney Company is still in the theme park business, bigger and better than ever, not only in California and Florida, but now in Japan, France, Hong Kong, and China, too.

Disneyland set a bar for job performance and work ethic against which I have measured every other career and customer service experience I have ever encountered throughout my life. My heartfelt thanks will forever go to Walt Disney and all the Disneyland cast and crew members for that incredibly important lesson.

Let's go back now to Southwest Airlines. I was eager to learn who Teresa Laraba held up on a pedestal as the epitome of Southwest values. When I asked her that question, her eyes instantly sparkled and she shined that beautiful, unforgettable, heartfelt smile of hers as she replied:

Oh, that's easy: Colleen Barrett!

I feel very fortunate to have had her as a mentor and someone who, over the last thirty years, I've had a chance to really get to know on a personal level. We share so much of the same values, not only professionally but personally. We came from a little bit of the same background, in how she grew up and how I grew up. I didn't really even know that until about twenty years into it, when we started working more closely together.

I always have respected her. She has always been the heart and soul of Southwest Airlines. When you actually get to know her and see how passionate and how personal the mission is for her—to really care for people—it is so genuine, you can't help but be driven by it and admire it. For somebody like me, it actually validates the fact you can be successful as you progress in a company and maintain those values. She's never compromised those.

Our employees have been raised to believe that is part of Southwest Airlines and there will always be somebody at the helm with a caring heart. I think that is why we've been successful and why the people who come after her are only successful if they extend that caring heart.

> **Her actions have always backed up the words she used. I think that is the key to what makes her different.**

I think what sets her apart is her values are lived. She started early on writing notes to people when there was a death or sending flowers at a good time or a bad time. I have had numerous opportunities over the years for her to reach out to me because of a difficult situation. Colleen cares so deeply and it is shown in how she exhibits her caring.

Let me give you an excellent example. I was diagnosed with breast cancer four years ago. I ended up having a double mastectomy. The first thing she did was reach out to me, to talk to me, because she also had breast cancer. It was years and years ago and she's obviously done fine. But she reached out to me, to talk to me about her experience, to let me know she was there for me if I needed anything. She sent food, sent handwritten notes. She came to the funeral home when I lost my mother.

Now she can't do that for forty-five thousand employees, obviously. But her actions have always backed up the words she used. I think that is the key to what makes her different. A lot of people can say they care, but then you don't see any action. You just hear the words. She backs it up with her actions.

"Would you call her a heartfelt leader?" I asked.

I don't know what else you would call her! I think she probably put the definition of "leading from the heart" and "having a servant's heart" especially in the airline industry. I would beg to say she's probably left that mark on corporate America, period.

Donald Stamets of Auberge Resorts actually began his hospitality career with the Westin Bonaventure Hotel in Los Angeles after he graduated college. During our dialogue, I asked Donald: "Was working for the Ritz-Carlton one of those opportunities where you thought 'If only I could just get to …?'"

Well, it's funny. I knew of them because I was a graduate from hospitality school. They tell you about the Four Seasons, the Ritz-Carlton and all that la-de-da. But I had never walked into one. I would always feel uncomfortable, raised on welfare and food stamps. I didn't really know what true luxury was.

In 1994, the year before I left the Bonaventure, the World Cup was in Los Angeles with Italy against Brazil. I was the convention services guy, doing a lot of parties for Colgate, Fuji Film in Italy and Brazil, and Coca-Cola.

So, I was doing all these parties. I was connected with a party planner in the city who, after the World Cup, called me to say, "I really want to thank you, Donald. I did parties all over the city and, by far, you were the best convention services manager I dealt with. You were timely, positive, and honest. I want to take you out to lunch to say thank you."

You ARE luxury, the way you treat people.

I was like, "Me?"

So I went on a three-hour lunch, martinis, and all. I'm at this point something like twenty-six years old and had never been to a three-hour martini lunch in all my life. This woman said, "You are amazing. You should work for Ritz-Carlton."

I said, "Me? I don't really know what luxury is."

She said, "It doesn't matter. You ARE luxury, the way you treat people."

"How did that make you feel?" I asked Donald.

Incredible! Like I could do it! That was the confidence I needed to go forward. You look at yourself in the mirror and go, "Really?"

I said, "Okay. I'm going to go for it."

So, I called the Ritz-Carlton in Pasadena. They only had a position available for a wedding manager.

I said to the director, "I appreciate it but I don't have that experience. I'm a corporate guy. If you had a convention services or corporate position available, I'd be very interested in interviewing. I appreciate it, but I'm going to pass because I know what my strengths and weaknesses are."

He said, "I appreciate your honesty. I like your spunk. I'll see what we have available elsewhere within the company."

I said, "That would be great."

Three or four days later, I get a call from the Ritz-Carlton in Rancho Mirage, California, in the desert. They said, "We have a corporate position available and we'd love to interview you."

So I drove out there for the weekend. I interviewed and got the position as the assistant director of convention services with Ritz-Carlton. I had a super-healthy tremendous career for fifteen years with them.

Intrigued to know more, I asked, "How old were you at this time?"

Twenty-eight years old.

"That's pretty amazing," I responded, "for somebody at twenty-eight to know your strengths and weaknesses."

> Yeah, that's a good point. I just knew at that time what I was really good at, and I wanted to make sure. You know, when you work with and you're trying to lead people, don't you really focus on the people and their strengths? I was really just doing that to myself. But maybe I didn't realize that, at the time. I was just focused. I knew what I was good at. I knew I was great at relationships and I was good dealing with the corporate world. So that's where I wanted to go. That was my focus.
>
> Down the line, I ended up doing weddings for Ritz-Carlton, believe it or not. I was good at that, too, eventually. I guess I needed to mature a little bit before I got there.

Skipping forward to his "getting there," Donald shared this about subsequent heartfelt leaders in his career who served as role models:

> Within Ritz-Carlton, Brian Gullbrants was an amazing leader. He currently is the executive vice president and managing director of the Wynn and the Encore in Las Vegas. He was my general manager at the Ritz-Carlton in Orlando back in 2003 and the opening general manager of that resort.
>
> He called me and said, "I can't open this thing without you, Donald." Actually, he called me Disco because that was my nickname. He said, "Disco, I cannot open this big monster without you. You need to be my convention services guy."
>
> I said, "Orlando? Really?"
>
> He said, "Dude, you're going to love it. Come on. This hotel is beautiful."
>
> So he flew us down there. We checked it out and, of course, I fell in love. I was there for six years and had three different positions in that hotel. I was the convention services guy. Then

when I was coming to the end of my career with convention services, I had done it for so long, I wanted to do something else.

I said, "I think I want to be a general manager."

He's the one who gave me the chance. The next day he said, "Okay. Do you want to be the food and beverage director, or do you want to be the rooms director?"

I scratched my head and thought, "You know, I've been in food for so long, catering and convention services for twelve years and then all those positions with Westin for six years."

I said, "I think I want to be the rooms director. Why not? Now remember, I only had that small little snippet of eighteen months as the front office guy at Westin twelve, thirteen, fourteen years ago, whenever that was."

He said, "Okay. I think you can do it."

Overnight I became the rooms director for the largest Ritz-Carlton in the company. We won so many awards in the two years I was rooms director for Ritz-Carlton. Our Ritz-Carlton was the most successful Ritz-Carlton back then.

We were connected at that time with the JW Marriott. We opened up this big Granite Links project together. It was very cantankerous between both companies because no more did the Ritz-Carlton people want to be "Marriott-ized" than the Marriott people wanted to be "Ritz-Carlton-ized."

But I'll tell you, Marriott has an amazing culture and back office and efficiency Ritz-Carlton could learn from. And Ritz-Carlton had the front of the house, and the service, and a culture Marriott could learn from. The teams were selected by Brian, and the general manager of the Marriott, Mr. Hoffman. We teeter-tottered each other.

Out of the gate, for the first three or four years, they were the best Marriott in the system and we were the best Ritz-Carlton in the system. It was awesome. Not many hoteliers will be able to experience what I experienced when we opened up Granite Links.

These are all inspiring messages, indeed. Yet I was even more intrigued to discover whether leaders who spend their careers in military environments might have heartfelt leaders as mentors. So, I asked retired Army Colonel Deb Lewis about her experience. She told me this:

Growing up, my father and mother were wonderful role models of people who led with a caring heart, and a heart for our country, always doing what was right by our country and for the greater good.

Two other people who greatly influenced me come to mind. One was really the first person to influence me once I left West Point and went into active service.

Most officers try hard to find somebody who can show them the way, show them the ropes. Otherwise, you may graduate from the academy, have all this education, and be an utter failure when you join an organization where you're responsible for people 24/7; involved in their lives, and potentially being in life-and-death situations.

Too many people misunderstand leadership in practice. Instead of leading from the heart, they may focus on controlling others, such as giving orders and forcing others to obey. This is the stereotype too many people think of regarding what it means to be "military." This couldn't be further from the truth for the best military leaders.

Without engaging our hearts, we may miss important opportunities to influence and positively impact others.

Someone who is hard on people, who never strays from strictly following and enforcing the rules, forgets the rules were made to improve situations in the past. Without engaging our hearts, we may miss important opportunities to influence and positively impact others. Those who fail to listen to the people around them often have a very difficult time later on.

I was lucky to have someone special to help me learn these things. He eventually rose to the rank of command sergeant major (CSM), which is the very highest enlisted rank. At the time we met, he was a sergeant first-class. His name was James O. Scott.

He epitomized what I think we hope to find in the military—a leader who was never afraid to dive into things which maybe were unpleasant but needed to be taken care of. He was one who worked with people, not just to observe them, but to give them a helping hand and also hold them accountable.

Being a heartfelt and positive leader doesn't mean you let everybody get away with everything. His way of taking care of them was to ensure they understood their responsibilities and carried out those responsibilities.

Scotty could read people's faces. I joked he could read people's minds when he would look at their faces. He could read the signs and he would do his best to help them. None of us could get away with being anything but authentic and honest with him. When people were "off," he would help them figure out what they needed. Or he might just help them, or inspire them, to do what they needed to do in the job. He did it by example.

What happens with heartfelt leaders is, they're capable of bringing out the best in you, and act like it was all you making it happen.

He died too young. He died right before my second major command. I do believe it was as a result of exposure during the first Gulf War, called the Gulf War Syndrome, where he traveled maybe a hundred thousand miles and was exposed to all sorts of chemicals, like anthrax, and was given many immunizations. I try to stay in touch with his family still and I let them know how much he meant to me. He was always there for me.

Like I said, he had another sense, a "sixth sense," to know if I needed to talk to him when he was alive. He certainly left a lasting legacy with his caring ways and in how much he did for other people.

The other person I have to mention is my husband, Lieutenant Colonel Douglass S. Adams (US Army, Retired). Although I'm sure he's the last person who would want me to talk about him.

I think what happens with heartfelt leaders is, they're capable of bringing out the best in you, and act like it was all you making it happen. There have been many times, when we are in leadership positions, you can care deeply. But sometimes you get slammed so many times, if you don't have someone else who understands what you're doing and why you're doing it, you might not be able to be successful without that assistance.

My husband continues to have a strong, positive influence on me. He also helped me realize we all have doubts. When we struggle, it is something good, not a fault in us. It means we are human, we care deeply when we continuously learn and choose to better ourselves. He reminds me I always have a good sense of what needs to happen in any situation: trust yourself and go forward because that's what you need to do.

Oftentimes, people get stopped by the tiniest negative feedback or self-doubt. I would say in all cases, the earlier examples I've given you, were people who helped me face adversity, to become stronger from each experience, and to see the opportunities often buried beneath hard work. They've made it possible for me to pass it on and positively impact more people. They've encouraged my passion to invite others in, help them be successful, too, and always strive to be even better, each and every day.

Engineers like to say "the road to success is always under construction."

When I first came to know Colonel Deb, I found it interesting the military might have heartfelt leaders. Of course, you may be thinking as I did, maybe because Colonel Deb is a woman, she sees things from a different perspective than a man in the military might. So I spoke to Todd Wilcox, chairman of Patriot Defense Group, to find out.

Todd, a decorated combat veteran, former CIA case officer, successful entrepreneur and business leader, founded Patriot Defense Goup in 2006, a defense contracting company dedicated to serving those who defend America. Todd also founded two other companies. Altogether, the combined business operations range from specialized security training for US special operations to defending corporate clients against cybersecurity attacks and the ground delivery of the US postal mail to our troops in Afghanistan.

Todd came to my attention as a heartfelt leader when he made a run for the United States Senate in 2016. I was immediately impressed when I met him.

With his macho military background, I figured I might hear a different kind of story from Todd than I had heard from Colonel Deb. When I asked him when, where, and from whom did he learn the values that have been most important to him throughout his life and career, Todd responded:

> It's really been a journey. It's been not just one person, or not just one place, or one time in which I learned the values that were most important, especially within the context of leadership. It's been "what to do" and "what not to do" that I've learned from people all along the way.

I've had a very unique experience. I've been in charge of or led almost every organization I've been involved in since I was twenty-three years old. I was in a fraternity. I was president of my fraternity for three years, then moved instantly into the military where I led a platoon in combat. Later, as a Special Forces officer, I was a Special Forces A-Team leader. In the agency (the CIA), I had several people who worked for me. I was a leader in my own organization there. As I grew up as a junior officer and then as CEO of the company I started, over the last eleven years or so, it's been a combination of things along the way that have shaped those values I think are most important in the context of leadership.

> **It wasn't just hard skill leadership lessons which I learned. It was empathy, emotional intelligence, understanding how people think and how they operate, and then being pragmatic.**

I'm a student, constantly trying to learn. You saw the quote when you came in, from Gandhi:

> **Live as if you're going to die tomorrow.**
> **Learn as if you're going to live forever.**

I'm constantly trying to learn and understand.

Along the way, it wasn't just hard skill leadership lessons I learned. Those are important as well. But it was empathy, emotional intelligence, understanding how people think and how they operate, and then being pragmatic. So, my leadership style is not authoritarian or hands-off. It's a combination. I've tried to develop, over time, a pragmatism.

I then asked Todd, "Do you think it's possible for people to lead that way if they're not at the top of the company?"

He replied:

Sure. The military espouses the best leaders are those who are good followers. So the leadership can be up and down the chain of command. Just because you're not in charge, overall in charge, doesn't mean you can't lead your seniors.

I've led from below the food chain, so to speak, several times. There, I think it takes even more patience because you don't have the authority to say, "This is the way we're going to do it." You have to influence them more. That goes to some of the heartfelt leadership I think you are talking about. It's the ability to influence people to buy into whatever your position is or whatever direction you might go.

While interviewing heartfelt leaders in various industries across the country, it was highly recommended I speak with the now former president of Texas Health Presbyterian Hospital in Dallas, Britt Berrett. His background includes both nonprofit and investor-owned environments in hospitals ranging from small to large. He has had a long career as a healthcare leader and administrator. Prior to joining Texas Health Presbyterian Hospital Dallas, he spent ten years as president and chief executive officer of Medical City Dallas Hospital.

Britt has indeed earned his reputation for strength in building physician stakeholder relationships and driving clinical operations to achieve outstanding business results.

He shared this story about some of the mentors who influenced his own heartfelt leadership style:

I could feel the genuineness of their love for me. There was no guile. There was no manipulation. There was no ulterior motive. They just cared about me.

I had a mentor at an early age, one who I just exchanged emails with this weekend, who does care about the individual and cares about me. He's followed me for twenty years now. A different personality than mine, and I think that's interesting.

Some folks are very charismatic, engaging, and warm. Others aren't. That's okay, but they do care about the team. Once again, the literature confirms that. Some people are a little more stoic and perhaps a little more introverted. Others are charismatic and wild and fun and loving.

The individual who comes to mind ... he cared about me. He cared about my profession. He cared about my family. There was a time in my life when I was a little out of balance with too much work and he realigned me. He was very kind about it, but he realigned me. I'm always grateful for that.

Another individual, probably twenty years my senior, retired, did the same. He wasn't in the business world. He was in my faith world. He kind of brought me back around to center, where I knew I needed to be.

Characteristics of those individuals? I could feel the genuineness of their love for me. There was no guile. There was no manipulation. There was no ulterior motive. They just cared about me.

I hope I've emulated that.

Soundbite FROM DR. MARK

To be the best you can be at any given moment, focus on what you are doing as if you will be doing this all your life. Give ALL your focus to it. Don't be distracted by other things or by what other people are doing. Just stay focused on what is in front of you and people will take notice. Ask yourself, "What is the most important thing I can do this year to impact the company's success?" Then, just focus on that and your performance will rise to the top.

ACTION STEPS

1 Think about your own experiences. When, where, and from whom did you learn the values that have been most important to you throughout your life and career?

2 What kind of bosses have you had? Did they manage up much more than they managed down and if they did, what effect did that have on you?

3 What effect would it have on you if you had a boss who would stand up for you when you can't, and even take a bullet for you in public; stand by you in a crisis and not let you fail; stand up to you in private, to push you to do things you didn't think you were capable of; and stand up to you, to stop you from doing something foolish that you would regret?

4 What kind of boss are *you*?

FIVE

It All Begins with You

What's most important to me is how we treat one another.
Then, as a leader, what has been entrusted to my care.
What it means to me is this: It's an opportunity for me
to choose greed or choose care and consideration.

—TIM HINDES
CEO of Stay Metrics

There are numerous maxims about creating your own success. Nelson Mandela gave us this one:

Learn to know yourself ... to search realistically and regularly the processes of your own mind and feelings.

Gandhi certainly had a few, including:

You must be the change you want to see in the world.

As human beings, our greatness lies not so much in being able to remake the world—that is the myth of the atomic age—as in being able to remake ourselves.

I especially like this one by Dr. Mark's very own mentor, Warren Bennis, scholar, organizational consultant, and founding chairman of the Leadership Institute at USC's Marshall School of Business:

Becoming a leader is synonymous with becoming yourself. It is precisely that simple, and it is also that difficult.

One I have had mounted big and bold behind my office desk and also hanging in my kitchen at home says this:

Attitude is everything. Pick a good one.

When I founded the leadership development company Business World Rising, I did so with a compelling vision to help high-potential individuals and the companies they work for take advantage of all the talent that already exists within the organization.

I am a firm believer we must look inside to challenge ourselves and manage ourselves in new directions every day. We must lead and behave in a way that we continuously inspire others to be all they can be, too. That, of course, is what this book is all about. Heartfelt leadership begins with you.

As I have shared with many mentees, the first step in your development as a leader is to identify what success means to you. Success does not lie in the achievement of what is important to others; others must achieve that for themselves. Accept you will never truly be happy, and you certainly will not make others happy, unless you are working toward achieving your own vision of success. That is where your spirit lies. It starts deep within you.

One of the most critical components of achieving success is having a clear understanding of where you are right now. Start from a solid foundation of self-knowledge. You must understand your flaws as well as your assets. Identify and embrace your strengths and your passions, your personal values, and your priorities. Only then can you move on to inspire others. Start with yourself.

It can be challenging to analyze yourself with clarity and objectivity. It can also be difficult to recognize your own strengths, especially if they come naturally to you. Some of us have been preconditioned to think we must work hard to develop our strengths. For this reason, we can sometimes be overly critical of ourselves and indifferent to our accomplishments. On the other hand, we may be overly confident in our abilities, have excess ego, and not honest with ourselves when it comes to acknowledging our own fears and fallibilities.

When Paul Spiegelman, cofounder of the Small Giants Community, was interviewed, Paul confided he was an introvert. Dr. Mark asked him to expand on being an introvert.

> I was always the quiet one. I think I was in kindergarten when my teacher said to my mom, "He doesn't say a lot, but when he does talk, it's like diamonds."
>
> I'm not outgoing. I'm not the center of attention. I'm the one who would rather be in my hotel room than at the cocktail party. I realize the power of good communication.
>
> Now I do forty speaking engagements a year. It's not that I can't get up there and speak, but I'm not looking to be the center of attention. I may be more reflective. It's just a part of my personality to be more on the introverted side and more measured in how I communicate with folks. That's just the way I was born.

Dr. Mark reflected, "You were formerly in a private company. For those ambitious people in publicly held companies, how can they make that leap to 'daring to care'? How do you change, to dare to care in a profitable way, so investors will want to invest in you?"

Paul responded:

> I think it's a little easier for me because I'm wired this way. I never knew any better. I never knew how to do it any differently. I've been doing this for many years. I have my own story to tell.
>
> The question, I think, is really for that leader who says, "This sounds interesting to me," or "I'd like to be that way," or "I'd like to run my company that way. How do I do it?" Maybe there's a big public company that hasn't run this way historically but wants to change. The leader says, "Well, how do I change? What's the road I go down because I'm used to doing it this way?"
>
> The first thing you need to do is be vulnerable. You need to sit down with your team. You need to talk about the fact you see a change needs to be made.

The first thing you need to do is be vulnerable.

Colleen Barrett, president emeritus of Southwest Airlines, shared these openly honest personal reflections and insights with me:

> My passion is customer service. It's not airline. It's not retail. It's customer service delivery.
>
> I'd never even heard of Servant Leadership until I read Peter Greenleaf's book ... and yet I think I was already a Servant Leader because I like to serve.
>
> I don't mean subservient. I like to serve causes. I want to serve and solve issues. I'm a firefighter. I don't have a ton of expertise in anything, but I will plug away at a problem for as long as I can stand it and try to come up with a solution.

I believe most issues can be solved if you study and work at trying to work together. Team playing, I guess.

I have a terrible—not correctable—depth perception problem. I've never driven a car, ever, for that very reason. If I got on the road, everyone else would have to get off. I can barely make it up and down stairs.

When all of my friends (especially when we got in seventh and eighth grade, freshman and sophomore year) were either cheerleaders or they were playing on sports teams or whatever, I couldn't jump and be a cheerleader if my life depended on it. I tried, and I couldn't do it. I was a klutz at that. I thought, "Okay. I want to be part of these things. I want to be part of the team, but I don't know how to do it."

That's how I got into it, thinking of ways I could be part of the support but not participating in what the sports were about. That's what I would start doing. I am a sentimental soul at heart so I'd start doing congratulatory cards. I'm not artistic or anything. But just things ... I'd plan the parties or whatever. That was my way.

I carried that into my job as a legal secretary. I didn't know what I was doing was unusual, particularly. I would see something I knew I could do. Why did my boss have to do it if I could do it? You almost have to teach a boss what you can do for him— and they were ALL "hims" back then — what you can do for them as a secretary because they don't get it.

At Herb's second law firm, which he formed himself, I became the office manager—with no title and no pay, by the way—to go along with it because none of them paid any attention to the nonlegal staff. It was a small firm, maybe sixty people. However, they would all come to me with their issues. So, I just became the office manager.

Somehow, I liked that. I could be impartial. I could see when people were trying to get something better for themselves. That's really where my values got put into play and where I saw how I could serve. Not to be subservient, but I could serve something good for the betterment of the whole versus the individual.

I never worried about pay or title, ever. Ever. I've always wanted to make a positive difference *and* I always wanted to be treated fairly. I didn't care if somebody made $2 an hour more than I did, as long as that person was contributing. What I didn't like was if someone was paid more and he/she wasn't contributing. That's about the only time I ever got bent out of shape. Again, I wouldn't go in and tell anybody they had to raise my salary. I would leave if I didn't think I was being treated properly. That taught me a whole, whole lot.

When I first moved to Dallas and started talking to our employees here, I remember lots of our couples would go up north to see the fall season or go skiing or whatever. So I would always give them my mom's name and phone number, and I would say to them, "I'm telling you, if you are going to Stowe, there's only one way to get there from Bradley or wherever, so you have to go through my home town. It's a tiny, tiny little place. You've got to call my mom. Here's my mom's name. Go to her house and ring the doorbell."

I had several of them do it, and they would come back and say, "Oh, my gosh. If you are a friend of Colleen's, then you are a friend of her mom's." That's just the way it was.

One kid was a ramp agent from San Antonio. He stayed with her for a week! By then, she was older and fairly disabled. Here's what tickled me to death: she didn't have anything, but she gave him little maps every morning. So, he would go out and go to these places she would tell him to see. Then he would come back and she would share dinner with him. He slept in one of the kids' bedrooms. That's just the kind of person she was. She was always open and welcome. She taught me all those things.

Mind you, during this conversation, Colleen and I were sitting in Colleen's office which, at the time, was right next to the office of the cofounder, chairman emeritus and former CEO of Southwest Airlines, Herb Kelleher. At this point during our interview, Colleen nodded her head and waved her left hand in the direction of Mr. Kelleher's office, continuing with some insights about him:

> He gives 110%. He is a truly, remarkably good human being. I think he is so smart—intellectually smart—he can't concentrate on the nitty, gritty details.
>
> He's very visionary. I'm not. He's very creative in his thinking. I'm not. But he is not a completer or a finisher. I am.
>
> We took the Myers-Briggs test, I don't know, twenty-five years ago. We took it with our whole department at the time, maybe about twenty or twenty-five people. The lady who administered it said, "I've been doing this all over the United States. I have never seen two people work as close together and who have rated as far apart as you two have on the last letter. You are 2,006 percentage points apart. I don't know how you haven't killed one another."
>
> I said, "Well, we shared the first three letters." I don't even remember what they are, but I remember the last one. It's Judgment versus Feeling, and that's the one we were so far apart on. Everything else we shared.
>
> I laughed, and I said, "Well, that's why we DO get along so well." Because I know what *my* weaknesses are. I try not to show them very often. I think Herb knows what his are, too, and he tries not to show them. So, we kind of shore each other up.

During the introspective conversation I had with Southwest Airlines' senior vice president of customers, Teresa Laraba, she shared this about taking stock of one's self:

You must be bold enough to ask some tough questions:

- Am I standing in the way of our success?
- Is there something I'm doing that is not allowing us to be successful?
- Are there ideas you have we haven't brought forward?

You have to tap into why the people you touch every day, first, think you're not being successful. Then it has to work its way all the way down.

Sometimes companies find it's the smallest thing they could be doing differently. They wouldn't know it unless they work their way to a frontline employee.

Many CEOs forget that. They look only at their C-suite. They look at only the people they see every day. They forget those who may be the lowest level individuals on that org chart, those who are delivering that service or that product. It could very well be that person who is making all the difference for you.

> **You must start with yourself. You must start by asking, "Where am I helping and where am I hurting?"**

You must start with yourself. You must start by asking, "Where am I helping and where am I hurting?"

Then you have to, through your leaders, get that pushed all the way down.

I asked Teresa why anybody would want to be a heartfelt leader. She responded:

Because of how much you are missing if you're not.

If you genuinely believe you are on this earth to make a difference in people's lives, and if you genuinely believe you're part of something bigger, but you are not a heartfelt leader, you are passing up an opportunity to meet some incredible people along the way and make a difference in people's lives in a way you'll never be able to articulate. You miss so much by not putting yourself out there.

I feel sorry for people who aren't willing to risk it because they'll never know the amount of gratitude and the fulfillment you can get personally and professionally if you do. It's worth every bump. It's worth every bit of pain.

I then followed up with, "What would you say to those who believe there is no room in the workplace for being heartfelt?"

Teresa had this to say:

Then you must have a really small workplace. You must have a really small mind.

If people do not care about what they're doing, I don't care if it's their job, or being a parent, or being a caregiver, there has to be something within an employee, within a person, that makes them care. If you don't think there is a place for that, I would question what makes you tick. What makes you care? Are you even showing the people with whom you work and live everyday what a difference it can make when the heart is part of the equation? It doesn't have to be the only part, but it has to be part of the equation.

We have an opportunity to employ many interns, and we get to speak with a lot of them. I have two children, one who is a nurse and one who is going to graduate this year. I give the same advice to my children that I give to our young leaders.

The corporate environment is different than it was probably when my parents were growing up. There is more of a corporate responsibility than there used to be. There is also a desire for employees to have a balance in their lives, more than there used to be.

I tell new prospective employees or anyone who's coming up:

- First of all, be willing to do whatever it takes. If you even start to say, "That's not my job," then you might as well finish that with, "I'm not going to be successful." Be willing to do whatever you can to make where you are successful and to show you're eager to do whatever it takes to be successful.

- You need to learn to be articulate. In the days of social media, you need to be able to actually verbalize what you think instead of just text and email what you think.

- You need to be able to be polished enough to present. It would also help if you remember that you have a personality. No matter what environment you're in, there's a good chance you can use part of that to convey your message. If you are in a more structured environment, then you will have to pick those opportunities and those times, but even in a structured professional setting, it doesn't mean there is no personality in it. At Southwest, we're an airline. If we aren't safe, then we have nothing. We take safety very, very seriously. That's not a joking matter. Thus, the other places where you can inject some personality, you should. In some different situations, you shouldn't.

> **Be willing to take on anything they ask you to do.**

- Be willing to take on anything they ask you to do.

- Learn to communicate effectively. Learn to show an engaging side.

- Teamwork. I think teamwork is more significant now than it ever used to be. You've got to be able to work on a team. Individual contributors are not as sought after as they were years and years ago.

- Also, find balance. Don't let your work life be your life. Find a balance because it will make you a better employee and it will make you a better person.

I then asked Teresa to comment on whether she ever felt indispensable. Here is her reply:

I want to think that if I left, I would leave a hole. I think I probably would for a day or two and then somebody else would run right in here and fill it up.

The fortunate part is, we are raised at this company to realize we are not indispensable, in the sense you should always have people who are working with you or for you who could take your place. The sign of a good leader is when you are gone, there is somebody ready to take your place.

I know I would leave a void, personally. I know some people would miss having me here, but I would like to think, professionally, I've done the responsible thing and Southwest Airlines would continue and would not miss what I was bringing professionally.

That's your responsibility. If you set yourself up to be indispensable, then when you are gone, people will question your leadership abilities when there's nobody there to pick up where you left off.

Next, I asked Teresa to define the characteristics of an indispensable employee. Here's what she had to say:

- Incredible follow-through;
- Timely follow-through; and
- A genuine connection with their team.

The leaders I've worked with, who have reported to me, who really connect with their teams and know how to get back to them when they have questions and help provide them the tools they need with the sense of urgency to do their job; these would probably be the top three skills.

It takes discipline to be excellent at follow-through. It takes discipline to have a sense of urgency to get your employees the tools they need. You can't do any of that if you haven't tapped into them.

> The most important feedback we get, as leaders, is when our employees don't feel like we follow back up with them.

Dr. Mark had the opportunity to interview Garry Ridge, Chairman and CEO of the WD-40 Company, maker of the ever-popular penetrating oil and water-displacing spray, WD-40.

A native of Australia, Garry has been with WD-40 since 1987 in various management positions. He has worked directly with WD-40 in fifty countries. In 2009, he coauthored *Helping People Win at Work: Don't Mark My Paper, Help Me Get an A* with Ken Blanchard.

In 2015, the Center for Leadership Innovation and Mentorship Building (CLIMB) named Garry its *Outstanding Business Leader for 2015*, citing him as a "walking textbook on effective leadership." We found him to be just that *and* a heartfelt leader to boot.

When Dr. Mark asked him, "When, where, and from whom did you learn the values which are most important to you?" Garry had this to say:

> It had to come from growing up in Sydney, Australia. My dad worked for one company for fifty years. Dad always used to say, "It's a fair day's work for a fair day's pay." I never saw Dad go to work without having his shoes polished and really setting an example. I think that was important.
>
> **Leadership is not about me, me, me. It's about how I am here to enable others.**
>
> I learned I was consciously incompetent, and I accepted that. I also learned I couldn't do everything. So I started to trust people. I sold newspapers when I was ten and eleven years old. I used to work on milk trucks. These people trusted me. I learned it's a two-way street.

You've got to realize it's not about YOU. Leadership is not about me, me, me. It's about how I am here to enable others, how I'm here to create an environment where people feel comfortable, where they don't feel threatened, where they don't feel fearful, where there's security.

This is a 24/7, 365 days a year leadership challenge. When we put on the badge of leadership every morning, we take on the responsibility of other people. As leaders, we have no right, by our actions, to mess up other people's lives. They do enough to mess up their own lives.

We leaders need to take that extremely seriously. Too many leaders out there, through their overinflated self, their ego, who are driven by short-term goals instead of long-term thinking, make decisions that hurt people every day. They have no right to do it.

The Dalai Lama says, "Our purpose in life is to make people happy. If we can't make them happy, at least don't hurt them." Our purpose as a leader is to help people engage and enable, NOT to hurt them. We want to apply to their positive, not to their negative.

It's just not right to put yourself in front of others for your own benefit and leave them on the sidelines. It's just not right.

I don't like self-centered leaders who do things to benefit themselves. We've got to put ourselves aside when it comes to that. In the end, we'll benefit.

Marshall Goldsmith tells a lovely story about interviews he did with people on their deathbed. They're talking about the greatest memories they had in life. It wasn't about the BMW or the corner office. It was about the people they had helped along the way. I got a lot of satisfaction out of that.

Nothing gives me more joy than to see someone whose arm I may have held for a short second in life, to go on and do wonderful things. As leaders, we have the opportunity to influence that because people are going to watch us. We've got to do what we say we're going to do. We've got to be there, in the moment, when people need us.

I'll tell you a funny story. When we were going through the global financial crisis in 2008, I observed people in the company as I'd wander around this office or any of our other offices around the world. People were asking me more often, "How are you?"

It dawned on me—they weren't asking me how *I* was; they were asking me how *they* were, through me. Now my answer to them could have been, "Oh, things are … ugh," or "Hey, let's not waste a good crisis. We're going to get through this. This, too, will end."

In hard times, as a leader, you need to be more visible than ever before.

I realized they were looking to me, in their time of uncertainty and fear, to give them that little bit of security to carry them through. Leaders need to make sure in times of war, and in times of trouble, they are visible.

At the same time, I lived downtown and went on a tour of the historic WWII aircraft carrier turned museum, the *USS Midway*. I found my way on to the bridge of the Midway. The tour guide was talking about the behavior of the captain on that boat. The captain had two residences on the ship. He had one below deck, which was a little larger area where he hung out. Then right up on the bridge, there was a bunk. In times of battle, he never left the bridge.

That taught me in hard times, as a leader, you need to be more visible than ever before. But how many leaders go underground in hard times?

That's why my people were asking me, "How am I?" (they weren't … they were asking me how *they* were). However, if I wasn't out there and visible, they'd say, "Hey, we're going through hard times. Where's our leader when we need him? We may want to ask him. We may want to engage with him."

You need to be up-front in times of trouble and in times of need, not hiding under some desk or locked away in some corner office.

I'm really fortunate. Somehow I'm genetically wired not to retain negative things for an extended time. If someone asks me the question, "Give me the worst experience you've ever had in your life," I'd have to think hard about it. If you say, "Tell me some elated moments," I can tell you about them immediately.

I say to my kids—who are actually adults—when they ask what I want as a gift, I'll say, "I want a memory." I'll never remember the tie you gave me two years ago, but I can tell you nearly minute-by-minute the great time I had when I went to Las Vegas with my daughter and my son. The three of us sat in the audience and watched Elton John at Red Piano. I can tell you when my son and I went to see Billy Joel or when we went to see Jimmy Buffett together. Why? Because it was surrounded by memories. So it's the positive side.

I think I've always been pretty positive. I find it hard to think negatively. I have on the bottom of my emails: "We all have something significant yet to do."

As Ken Blanchard says, "Life is a very special occasion. Don't miss it." We live in ten-second intervals. So why not do the best you can in each one of those ten seconds. Does that say I don't get down in the dumps and I don't have times when I get a little frustrated? Of course, I do. I'm human. However, I think I'm much more on the other side.

When Dr. Mark interviewed Howard Behar, the former president of Starbucks Coffee disclosed how he went through his own process of self-discovery following his confrontation with the CEO of the company he worked for early in his career. These were some of the questions he asked himself:

What were my values? What did I want to accomplish in my life? What did I want to leave behind? Who was I? Who was Howard, in fifty words or less?

That has really formed my life.

I listed out my core values. I thought about what my mission might be. At that time, it was a pretty basic mission. I was working in the home furnishings business and I wanted to be known as one of the best leaders in the home furnishings industry.

Sometimes people need to break down before they can break through.

Over time, it changed to what it is today: I want to nurture and inspire the human spirit every day, beginning with myself first and then for others.

My ex-boss actually gave me a gift when he put me in that pain. Alternatively, it was my response to what he had said during my confrontation with him. I decided I didn't want to do that again. So, the gift was forcing me to take a look at myself and decide who I was, what I stood for. That began this journey of figuring out who Howard was and trying to live a life according to Howard.

When Dr. Mark prompted, "Sometimes people need to break down before they can break through," Howard responded:

Well, I certainly felt that way, no question about it. I had made my decision to resign from my job—a job I had loved—only three or four months before that. I went home one night and said to my wife (she was only two months away from giving birth to our daughter, Serena), "I have to quit."

We had no money saved. We had no way of really doing anything. Here I was, saying I was going to quit my job. I was trying to escape. I just wanted to get out of it. I just wanted to get away as fast as I could. The only way I thought I could do that was to quit the job, to get out of there; to run, in essence.

I felt guilty. I felt stupid. I felt like I was never going to amount to anything. I was never going to be a good executive. Over time, the more I talked with people about what I'd gone through, somebody gave me a book on how to think about myself. I don't even remember the title anymore. It was those people who were there for me when I needed it, and books.

I started on that little search. One step led to another. I remember getting this book. The book said, "The first thing we want you to do is to look at your core values. What are they?"

I'd never thought about what my core values were. So, I started doing that work. It was tough. It was really hard because there was this list of three hundred words. I was trying to figure it out. The book said you had to get it down to about eight. Eight from three hundred? It was tough.

I gave it up, and then I came back to it. You know, it was a herky-jerky process. It wasn't like I came out of it and went on this path to being a healthy human being. It's been up. It's been down. Now I'm almost seventy years old, and I still work on it. I still think about it. There's no end to it.

What I have learned is, even on my grayest of days—and we all have gray days—they don't last forever. I used to think I was the only one who had gray days. I'd think, "I'm having a gray day. There is something wrong with me." The days would last, and I couldn't get rid of them. I was

There are times when you can't control things. Sometimes you must let go.

fighting against them. But over time I figured out, the less I fought it but rather accepted it: "Howard, you're having a gray day. It's okay," the faster they went away.

I realized I'm just a part of it. It doesn't mean I haven't had times with depression again. I have. It doesn't mean I haven't had struggles. I have. But over time, I started to gain confidence. As my mother used to say: "This, too, shall pass." She was right. It always passes.

Dr. Mark reflected, "Sometimes successful people try to control things, but there are times when you can't control things. Sometimes you have to let it go."

Howard responded:

> It's an odd thing. But when you let go, when you release, when you're struggling with that kind of issue, when it's a gray day, or whatever it happens to be, or whatever you happen to be struggling over, you kind of take your arms around it, and you grab it and you hug it. You pull it close to you. You give it love. I know it's an odd way to think about it. The minute you do that, all of a sudden, there is nothing there. It disappears.
>
> I'll give you an example that happened to me. When I retired from Starbucks the second time, it was a struggle for me. I was trying to let go of a place that was dear to me. It wasn't a job. Everything about it represented my values. Everything I believed in was in that place and the people.
>
> So here I am, not working anymore. I'd come off the board. I was disappointed with some things. Whatever it was, it didn't make any difference. I spiraled. Every night I would go to bed, thinking about Starbucks. I'd wake up in the morning, thinking about Starbucks.

Your life's work is still your life's work.

> I knew it wasn't healthy. I wasn't a kid anymore. I kept saying to myself, "Howard, move through this. Move through this." I was thinking I was doing all the things to move through it. "Howard, you'll get over this. This will pass." All this self-talk was going on, but it just didn't seem to go away. I kept trying to replace Starbucks. I needed to replace those passions and that purpose that went along with that, being part of that kind of organization.
>
> One day I was lying on the sofa, reading a book. My thoughts were going in and out of it. I was kind of chastising myself a little bit. I closed my eyes and exhaled, deeply. Then, into my

brain came words. I'll never forget that time, just lying there. The words were these: "Howard, your life's work is still your life's work. Howard, your life's work is still is your life's work."

I heard those words. I started repeating them to myself, just lying there on the sofa. For a week, every day, I'd get up and have a little struggle. I'd start repeating those words. I mean, it was like magic. Within about two weeks, all of a sudden, doors began opening everywhere—things I had been blocking because I hadn't been able to release—all of a sudden because I realized, "Yeah, my life's work is still my life's work."

Do I love Starbucks? Did I love what we did there and the values it represented? Yes. But, you know, Starbucks was not me, and I wasn't it, as much as I was a part of it, and it is a part of me. My life's work was my life's work before I went to Starbucks.

That opportunity and those words made a huge change. But it's that kind of hugging, hugging, and hugging it. As soon as you hug it and caress it and love it, it seems to lose all its power.

When I interviewed Britt Berrett, former president of Texas Health Presbyterian Hospital in Dallas, here's how he responded to my $64K question: "When, where, and from whom did you learn your values?"

I think the foundation of my leadership behavior is my faith and my family. There's no question about it.

I just had a profound life experience. I took two years of my life and served as a missionary. I lived in Peru for a couple of years. Most of my life has been outside the United States. My dad had been a missionary in Uruguay. We had a family tradition of that.

I remember asking myself: "What's it all about, Alfie?" "Why am I here?" "Where did I come from?" "Where am I going?"

One responsibility I had in Peru was to tour through hospitals and provide blessings to those who were injured and in need of a sense of faith. It broke my heart to see how those who were infirmed, those who were sick, and those who were incapacitated, how the community treated them. It broke my heart, and I thought, "There's got to be something more to it."

In that environment, I was teaching my faith in Christ. But I looked at how they treated people in health care. When I returned to the United States, and I decided to select a career, I thought, "I'm not good at clinical. I'm not. However. I've got a good business mind." That's what drew me to my profession.

Interestingly enough, I was kind of alone in that. I went to grad school and came out of grad school and worked for a system (I studied health administration and went to medical school in St. Louis). I was kind of alone in that passion, but you find people along the way.

When I was a kid, we used to go crabbing. I lived in Canada. What we would do is get a canoe and get a stick with a bunch of wires around it, a fishing line, in about three or four feet of water. You would paddle around, and you'd see the crabs chasing around in the sand. That's what we'd do. It was a lot of fun. You'd catch them, and you'd have a big crab bake.

However, my dad taught me something important. His lesson: one crab in a bucket will escape. Two crabs, three crabs won't escape. The reason being, as one crab tries to emerge, the other crab will grab its leg and pull it back down. So until you have two or three crabs in the bucket, you could potentially lose them. Once you have those three crabs in that bucket, they'll all pull each other down. That was the metaphor or the analogy I used in life as I'd talk with folks: there was this tendency and behavior of pulling one another down.

I saw, in the early part of my career, where people would begin to emerge. They'd care about a team. They would extend themselves. But their peers would pull them back down. They'd say, "You can't do that. You get too close, and you can't be objective."

I thought to myself, "Why shouldn't I care about my team? Why shouldn't I care about their personal and professional lives?"

"No. Time out. You get too close, and then you compromise that professionalism."

I'm thinking, "I'm not sure that's true." I'm not talking about enabling. I'm not talking about condoning. What I'm talking about is caring and loving them, hoping for the best.

Sometimes it means they are not in the right position. Or perhaps they don't have the correct skill set. Or maybe they need some coaching or some mentoring. Maybe they need to coach and mentor *me*. Maybe how they're doing it is the right way to do it. Maybe I need more humility.

I still remember, I was an assistant administrator and a new CEO came on board. He observed me for maybe a couple of weeks. He brought me to his office, sat me down, and said, "Listen, you need to act the part. Even if you're not the part, you have to act that way. You need to project an image." He'd use all these buzz words: You have to "project an image" and "present yourself in such a way."

I'm thinking, "I'm not so sure that's right. I think I need to be who I am, and I need to be with people who I care about. If I don't love them, then I need to figure out how to love them." He and I just didn't sync. So I left, and I'm glad I did.

That's how I proceeded. I found at every turn, when I cared about the team, I began with the core of people who directly reported to me. Then I went to those who reported to them, and then the staff as a whole. I started small, with small entities. I was recognized for successes in a small hospital. Later, as we grew, it became even more dramatic because people are thirsting after this leader who cares about them, who is willing to invest her/himself in their success.

History confirms it time and time again: being a heartfelt leader, caring and loving, is powerful.

I think being a heartfelt leader is powerful. It's what drives success. If you don't believe me, pick up some books on leadership, and it'll confirm. Look at the "Best Places to Work" and what they call Level Five or Five-Star Leaders. They care about the team. They really do care. They are heartfelt. Is it exhausting? Yes, sure, no question. Is it rewarding? Absolutely. I guess I don't accept that as an excuse. I think loving and caring for your team is foundational and core to leadership.

Think about all the great leaders out there, the ones who have sustained the test of time. Take a look at Moses, for crying out loud. He loved the children of Israel. He absolutely loved them. He loved his God. He was willing to do everything to bring them out. He even knew he wasn't going to go to the Promised Land. He knew he was going to lead that organization, three million children of Israel, the Israelites, across the Red Sea. He was not going to enjoy the success, but he loved them so much he was willing to pay the price.

You see these great leaders. The ones who don't care, their tragedies are historic. I guess it sounds a little altruistic, but history confirms it time and time again: being a heartfelt leader, caring and loving, is powerful. It's what successful organizations enjoy.

I asked Todd Wilcox, former Green Beret and Special Forces A-Team commander, what kind of things were most important to his success:

You've got to be honest with yourself.

Just being grounded, but I think that's come out in our dialogue. Just being grounded in understanding who you are, I believe, is critical to being able to lead people. If you don't know who you are, I don't think you can effectively lead others.

You've got to be honest with yourself. Having the wife I have, who is very candid, who praises my successes and is open about the areas of improvement I need to work on, that helps.

That's been pretty critical along the way: being able to know who I am so I can effectively lead the people around me.

Going back to the fact I like to read, and I like to learn along the way, I brought the book in today, *Good to Great*. A lot of business people have read it. It's one of the best-sellers of all time in terms of professional development-type tools. In there, they describe a Level Five leader.

There's a chapter where Jim Collins took a very analytical approach to analyzing companies that went from good to great, the aspects that made them successful and different from the others. One of them was what he called Level Five leadership.

It was a description of where I thought I'd been when I started reading it. There were a few things I was lacking, and I learned to try to develop those things over time:

- You're more of a workhorse, not a show horse

- You're not ego-driven

- You attribute the success (he uses an analogy of a window or a mirror), you attribute out, through the window, the success of what's going on

- When you fail or when the organization fails or stumbles, you see yourself in the mirror. You take responsibility for it.

That had a little impact on the development of my leadership style, as well. At the time I read it, I thought, "Man, that's me." There were a few things I was missing, but I've tried those out and honed them along the way. So, that influenced my leadership development, too.

I then asked Todd, "Can you think back to a time in your life when you weren't that way?"

Yes, certainly. In the military.

I was a brand-new second lieutenant in the infantry, in the 101st Airborne Division, developing my skills.

You had noncommissioned officers, sergeants, who were much more seasoned and experienced than you were as a brand new lieutenant fresh out of college, coming out of ROTC.

There were times where I thought, "This is the military," like you said, that stereotype of hard charging, "it's my way or the highway" kind of stuff. That didn't always play well, certainly when you have no experience as a young adult, and you're saying, "This is the way we're going to do it." That doesn't always set well with an NCO (noncommissioned officer) who's been around for quite some time and who says, "Humm. There might be a better way to do this, Lieutenant," and off he goes.

I got bumps and bruises and some scars from those kinds of interactions with very senior NCOs who were trying to mentor me. I was a bit reluctant at the time, thinking, "I don't want to show any weakness. I've got to know what direction we're going and I'm going to lead from the front."

So, there were some experiences along the way, in the military.

Probably the same is true here in corporate America, as we teamed with other big companies to go after big projects or got into complex situations because we do a lot of unique services across all three business units. There were probably sometimes where we were working with people who probably knew better than I how to get things done. Maybe I wasn't as collaborative as I should have been.

Yeah, there have been some lessons along the way.

Heartfelt leadership taps into our richest source of personal power.

When I followed up with "You're never too old to learn," he replied:

Hopefully not.

Military pioneer retired Colonel Deb Lewis spent thirty illustrious years with the United States Army. I queried Colonel Deb to find out whether a female officer might offer a different perspective on what it takes to be an exemplary heartfelt leader.

> Heartfelt leadership was not a term with which I was familiar. I would say caring about others is something that came naturally to me, genuinely caring about who you were working with, and caring deeply about our mission and what we were accomplishing, although it helps to be reminded from time to time.
>
> I remember getting ready to give a speech as part of an earlier change-of-command ceremony. I was very stressed over what I was presenting. Someone gave me the best tip ever, one I live by to this day. They said, "Speak from your heart, and everything will be great." These tips—I like to call them Rapid Positivity Remedies—are something I love to collect and pass on because they are life-changing, simple to recognize and cure us of unhelpful habits in an instant.
>
> For me, it was a really compelling message. It resonated with who I wanted to be in every way. When I was in front of other people, I'd been trained to focus on the logic and the facts, or some specific message.
>
> Heartfelt leadership taps into our richest source of personal power. It's a very positive and perpetually energizing place that recognizes and ignites that power in others.
>
> When you have a heartfelt leadership style, you may not be "welcomed" by everyone, and you may even be regularly attacked. In my case, it was clear my peers and subordinates understood I was doing my best and trying to make a positive impact. Their feedback would gird me and make it easier to survive "leaders" who believed they were helping, but their actions reflected a greater concern for "looking good" or not making waves, no matter the negative impacts on others.
>
> Even under the best of conditions, any of us can be quickly brought to our knees by a circumstance, by a setback, by a whole host of things that can happen. I certainly have had

far more than my fair share of times where I've questioned everything about who I am. Even if the people are out there to help you, they may not be enough to give you the strength you need.

Anything I'd like to have that's different than I have now has to start with me.

Pay attention and you'll find any number of people who have been in the same boat, or a similar situation. Even when you fall short, it's never too late to change how you look at your circumstances, how you deal with the people in your life. Some wake up much later than others to discover their greatest power resides within them. Maybe it's something they've read, or perhaps a person who has come into their life they can look up to, who helps model that behavior which reflects who they want to be.

Being a heartfelt leader is important for our happiness, to realize you can and are making a difference. Being a heartfelt leader is setting aside ego.

Soundbite FROM DR. MARK

Breakdowns precede nearly all breakthroughs.

To keep those breakthroughs making you stronger, better, and more successful, the secret is to keep saying to yourself when you're in the middle of a breakdown, "This is a breakdown. You will survive it, and it usually leads to a breakthrough. Now don't do anything to make it worse for seventy-two hours."

The next and equally important step—after allowing your breakdown, recentering and becoming ready to reengage the world effectively—is to pause and say to yourself, "Now what?" At that point, think of what outcome you want to accomplish, in the near-term and long-term, then select the milestones to achieve to get there, and finally, what you will need to do to reach those milestones.

ACTION STEPS

1 Think about what makes you tick. Don't be modest. Don't be apprehensive. Be honest.

2 Write down your strengths.

3 Find out if your list of strengths matches what others see as your strengths. Ask your spouse or life partner, your parents or siblings, your peers, and your staff what they see as your greatest strengths.

4 Write down your shortcomings.

5 Find out if your list of shortcomings matches what others see as your shortcomings. Ask your spouse or life partner, your parents or siblings, your peers, and your staff what they see as your biggest gaps.

6 Now define your passions.

7 Write down your personal and professional values.

8 List the real priorities in your life, in order.

9 Now, consider what you must do to live a life without regrets.

SIX

Lay a Foundation of Trust

Trust is the glue that makes the world go around.
Without it, nothing can happen.
—HOWARD BEHAR
former President, Starbucks Coffee

Dr. Mark may be too humble to ever say this about himself, but he just might be the world's preeminent expert on listening.

As I alluded in the first chapter, I didn't even know Dr. Mark when I first read his now international best-selling book, *Just Listen*. While *Just Listen* is technically categorized as a business and self-help book, when I read it that very first time, I was convinced it was the best diagnostic leadership book I had ever read.

Based on my decades in high-tech sales, management consulting and leadership, not to mention being a daughter, wife, mother, and leader of several civic and social organizations, I can honestly say I have found effective listening—listening with the intent to gain true understanding—to be the single most essential skill to master for heartfelt leaders. Listening to understand builds trust.

Former IBM chairman Sam Palmisano once gave this reason when asked why his experience working in Japan was so important to his own leadership development:

> Because I learned to listen. I learned to listen by having only one objective: comprehension. I was only trying to understand what the person was trying to convey to me. I wasn't listening to critique or object or convince.

As Dr. Mark stated on the dedication page of his book *Just Listen*, it was his mentor, friend, and inspiration Warren Bennis who taught him when you "deeply listen" and get where people are really coming from, and then care about them when you're there, they're more likely to let you take them where you want them to go.

Followers who tell the truth,

and leaders who listen to it,

are an unbeatable combination.

— WARREN BENNIS
American scholar, organizational consultant and author

In my now well-worn, dog-eared, and underscored hardbound copy of *Just Listen*, one of my most favorite sections is entitled "Why Does 'Feeling Felt' Change People?" It says:

> Making someone 'feel felt' simply means putting yourself in the other person's shoes. When you succeed, you can change the dynamics of a relationship in a heartbeat. At that instant, instead of trying to get the better of each other, you 'get' each other, and that breakthrough can lead to cooperation, collaboration, and effective communications …

... showing you understand, accept how the person feels and you'd feel the same, you make these frightened clients 'feel felt.' When people feel felt, they feel less alone, and when they feel less alone, they feel less anxious and afraid—that opens them up to the message you are trying to send. They shift from defensiveness ('Get away!') to reason and they're capable of hearing your message and weighing it rationally.

To create and maintain an open, inclusive, and trusting environment, the next most important thing to do is honor and respect one another. You do this by showing genuine interest in the other person and demonstrating you believe their intentions are honorable.

Of all the things I learned at IBM, the thing that meant the most to me—something I have carried with me in all the years ever since and one of the core foundations of my own personal leadership philosophy—was IBM's principle of *Respect for the Individual*. This IBM basic belief, *Respect for the Individual*, respect for everyone's rights and dignity, stemmed from these three foundational principles that leaders should:

- Help each employee to develop their potential and make the best use of their abilities

- Pay and promote on merit, and

- Maintain two-way communications between manager and employee, with opportunity for a fair hearing and equitable settlement of disagreements.

When IBM managers ceased to uphold these principles, things began to fall apart. Nevertheless, no matter where my career took me after I left IBM, my own continued adherence to IBM's basic belief, *Respect for the Individual*, never failed me. I am grateful the values of founder Thomas J. Watson were instilled in me fairly early in my career. It was a valuable lesson learned to experience firsthand how quickly trust can erode when such values are cast aside.

Interested in discovering the kind of core values and business philosophies other best places to work practice, Dr. Mark and I elicited insights from each of our now-familiar heartfelt leaders regarding how they went about building open, inclusive, trusting, and respectful environments within their respective organizations.

First, let's hear from one more best-ever boss, Reinhold Preik, retired founder and CEO emeritus of Chemcraft International, a leading global manufacturer of innovative industrial wood coatings.

As a young boy, Reinhold (commonly referred to as Rein) grew up in East Germany before the beginning of World War II. His tale of living through Hitler's regime in a country torn apart by horrific conflict would send chills up your spine. By the grace of God, Rein and his boyhood family survived forced evacuations, the Russian invasion, his father's capture by Russian soldiers, and more.

Ultimately, he and his family walked hundreds of miles on foot to return to their pre-war home in Berlin. Once back in Berlin, little Rein was reenrolled in school. His old school building was partially bombed out. Half the roof and the glass were gone, so they moved the school to a pub. He advanced to the sixth grade and went on to school through grade ten, when he entered another school, preparing him to become a paint chemist. Two years later he graduated and emigrated to Canada on a quest to escape the Communist system.

When I asked Rein how he became so successful after such a horrendous childhood, he told me:

> I applied to a large paint company in Canada. They hired me as a research technician in the polymer area of the business. I worked there for five years.
>
> I had an opportunity to start a job in the same field with a startup company. Then it was a matter of progression and performance. Somebody would leave, the company grew, there was a reshuffling, and I became general manager of the company. After being general manager for a year or two, I became the president.
>
> It's not that easy to break away and start your own business. One of the motivating factors for me was that the owners were negotiating to divest themselves of the company. Looking at new owners in the future helped me to make the decision to do it on my own. I really wanted to try to see if I could do it. It's something you just want to do.

Eventually Rein established another industrial coatings firm. He went on to say:

> I made a deal with a Danish company in which they became minority partners in the business. We became fairly strong in a very small area of the specialty coatings business. Over the years we became well accepted and well-known, and the company grew quite substantially.

When I asked Rein, "Was it a natural move for you to go from being a research technician to a more people-oriented role?" he responded this way, with his still distinctly German accent:

> You know, I never thought about this. Some things you just do. As far as handling people, what's important is to have trust. It's all a matter of trust. People have to trust you, and you have to trust the people.

Now, in this situation, when you already have a structure, the dynamics are a little different. When you start a business like I did, the dynamics are different than when you work for somebody. When you have that structure in place, you have to work within the structure.

At that time, we were a fairly small company so the number of employees was not great. But when you hire people, I think the key is that you are honest and upfront with them. I don't think people want surprises, particularly negative surprises. So, it was really up to me to hire people, given the partner was really out of the operating business.

I went on to ask Rein, "What did you do differently to foster loyalty with people?"

I think, first, you've got to be straight and honest with them. You have to trust them, too. It's a two-way street.

Everyone wants to be successful ... If you can help them be successful, they'll be your friends for the rest of your life.

Once you trust them and you assign to them an area of responsibility within the business, you have to let them perform. You've got to look at their performance, not "how do you walk" but "you do walk." You know what I'm saying? I think we've been very successful because we allowed people to develop their own style.

We had somebody who was in charge of the Quebec business once. He was a totally different person. His background was different. His approach to business was different than someone who would have been in the United States. But you've got to accept that. Don't try to make everybody the same. I think the company will lose a lot of color and a lot of personality if you do that.

Of course, you also have to sell yourself, so they can feel they can trust you. When they ask you for something, you're going to be there. When there is a problem, you are going to be there and you're not going to leave the customer stranded because you haven't fulfilled your promise to them. Then, of course, I did a lot of traveling to get a good feeling for the area, for the culture.

In the end, everyone wants to be successful. You have to keep that in mind. It doesn't matter which language they speak, what clothes they wear, what color their skin is. They want to be successful. If you can help them be successful, they'll be your friends for the rest of your life.

The way I looked at it, and we tried to get this philosophy through the company, is to just show them what kind of job we needed done. We were not trying to tell them exactly how to do it. Just tell them what kind of job you need done.

Like, "Here, you've got a dirty floor." I bring in a broom and I tell him, "I have two or three brooms. The room is dirty and you need to sweep it." I'm not going to tell him which broom to use. That's going to be up to him. He's going to choose the right broom and he's going to get the floor clean.

That's kind of simplistic, but in business it's a similar situation. If you tell someone exactly how you want it done, then you're controlling the whole thing and it gets very difficult. You're going to run out of steam.

I then asked Rein, "Where do you think *pay* versus *creativity* comes in and is loyalty important?"

I don't think you can have one without the other. They are linked together. People know you are not just in it for yourself, but you are in it for them as well. It's obvious they are coming to work for me, but sooner or later, they realize they are in it for themselves as well.

Of course, pay is very important. You would like to see them grow. You would like to see them grow in their personal lives as well, and with their family life. Pay is important, but it's not that important in the sense people will leave you to go somewhere else. They will realize, wherever they go, it still comes down to their performance.

If you, as a leader, help them perform, then they are going to be happy themselves. Their self-worth is going to be there. If people have self-worth, they are going to be happy. If they are working in a place where they don't feel self-worth, they don't feel the company really cares who they are ..."they don't really care what I am doing, I'm just punching the clock, I'm going home and nobody even knows I'm here"... then their attitude is going to be completely different.

When I asked, "How did your people know you cared about what was important to them?" Rein responded:

Well, we would have several get-togethers each year with the employees. For instance, for Christmas we would make sure their whole family was there. We would make an effort to take people (those who had responsibilities for certain areas) somewhere. One year we went to France. One year we would go to England with their spouses. We fostered a pretty close relationship with them.

Curious about that, I asked, "Did you do that as an award or was it something you did for your entire leadership team?"

I wouldn't say it was as an award. It was more to get a bond between the people. If you do it for a reward, there may be some people who had performed better than some others, but that doesn't mean the others wouldn't have a future.

I think it's important they learn from each other as well. If you give them an opportunity to learn from each other, then when you get them together and socialize together, then you will find they are willing to help each other. You just get more of a family-type of a feeling within the company. It happens when you operate that way. That's the outcome.

Paul Spiegelman of the Small Giants Community had this to say when Dr. Mark commented, "It seems the world conspires to make people feel like 'nobodies.' Yet it seems you are about making people feel like 'somebodies.' Is that so?"

I would tweak that a little bit. I would say everybody is a "somebody." We're not taking "nobodies" and making them feel like a "somebody." We're recognizing they *are* "somebody."

I think that's what I've been able to do. I never aspired to that. I just found a way to build relationships with

The key to building relationships with people is making them feel good about themselves.

people. I think the key to building relationships with people is making them feel good about themselves. Whether that's an employee or someone else I did something with in business, a customer, a vendor, in each of us there are good things we've done. Each of us wants to talk about it.

I can ask people questions. I can learn enough about them and show I care about them to make them feel good about themselves. To me, that is probably the secret sauce, so to speak: make people feel good about themselves. People are inherently good.

Even in our company, when we have those naysayers or negative influencers, I talk about the courage we need to make tough decisions, to move people on in their businesses. But it's not their fault. It's our fault. We hired them to begin with. What was the mistake we made in not seeing something?

Yet everybody, I believe, at the heart of it, is a good person. People want to succeed. We may have an environment that's not the right environment for them. But that doesn't mean they can't be wonderful in the next place they go.

There's obviously that percentage of people who maybe don't belong in our company or they don't belong in the next company, but those are few and far between. Most people are good people with good hearts, who want to do good things, feel good about themselves and take care of their families. I give all of them the benefit of the doubt.

I hope I can allow people to pause and feel good about what they're doing. When you're in a position of influence or power, then that has even more impact. That's something, I think, as leaders we don't take advantage of enough.

When I can send a personal note card to someone's home or make a call on a Sunday because someone's got kidney stones, and it means so much to the person that I'm told about it years later. And what did it take me? Thirty seconds to write, address, and mail that note to their home. You could change somebody's life.

**I don't know.
What do you think?**

When you have a position of influence over others, if you can use that tool, I think that's the best thing you can do. The business will come. They'll work hard for you and you'll build relationships for the rest of your life.

We are all on this journey together. Nobody is perfect. We all are challenged to keep that level of genuineness over time, in every relationship we build, and with everyone we meet.

You need to be inclusive with your team, to do this together. You need to listen to them and use their ideas.

William Marriott had what he called the seven most important words in business: "I don't know. What do you think?"

As leaders, we tend to think we know the answers and many times we might. But if we step back for a moment and be patient and wait for those answers to come from other people, implement those ideas, give them credit. Oh my gosh, what a difference you're going to see in the team you're building, in how they feel about their work and how fulfilled they are in their lives. It's got to be an inclusive exercise.

Dr. Mark asked Paul, "Is there a difference between being *nice* and being *kind*?" Paul responded this way:

> I think so. As I would describe being nice, I think being kind might even be a deeper level. Nice is something you can simply be, purposefully. Kind might be something more deliberate. You are really taking the time to care or think about that person versus just simply on the surface being nice to them.
>
> I had a wonderful compliment recently from the head of our HR department, who has been with us for six years. My company was just sold and he decided to move on in his career. He sent me a note and he said, "You taught me something very important in my life. You taught me kindness." That made me feel good.
>
> So, I think there probably is a difference. For someone to be kind, I think, is to really go beyond just being nice to them, or being friendly. It's hoping you are giving them something more.

Drilling a bit deeper, Dr. Mark asked, "Would you say being *nice* is what you do and being *kind* is who you are?"

> Yes. I think that's who I aspire to be.
>
> I think being kind is when someone feels they got something more from you. You taught them something or you delivered something. You enhanced their life.

Dr. Mark had a similar conversation with Garry Ridge of WD-40. During their dialogue, Garry posited:

I think if you can have those kinds of candid conversations with people in life, you can say to them, "I mean you no harm. I'm here. You can take what I'm going to share, you can do what you like with it." But it's not about me wanting to harm you. It's about me wanting you to be in a position where you can perform your own personal magnificence on a daily basis because you're free. You're moving from fear to freedom.

The reason people leave organizations is because they feel they don't belong. I love Maslow's Hierarchy: Safety, Security, Survival. The next one is Belonging. Companies forget that. How many parties or social functions have you left because you didn't feel like you belonged? How many relationships are broken because one party didn't feel like they belonged?

The Learning Moment is taking away the fear of failure.

So, what we've got to do, through Care, Candor, Accountability, Responsibility, Respect, Learning, and Teaching is—in an organization—create this organization where people truly feel like they belong. When they belong, they will find meaning in their work.

So it's not about being happy. It's being meaningful. So once they're creating meaning in their work, the work becomes more meaningful to them. They feel like they make a contribution to life. They do great work. You celebrate that. You have fun and organizations grow. It's simple.

When you talk about the Learning Moment, the Learning Moment is taking away the fear of failure. The biggest demotivator we have in life is fear, when we're afraid to do something. So, when people are afraid, they absolutely cut down their opportunity to be creative. The Learning Moment is about taking that fear away so people can share in an open and honest way.

The Learning Moment is a bit like when some people talk about Servant Leadership. Servant Leadership is not about the prisoners running the prison. The Learning Moment is not about being soft. You have to be tough-minded *and* tenderhearted. The genius is in the *and*."

So how do you get that balance between toughness and tenderness that allows people to not only learn, but to benefit from that learning? By taking that learning into something new. It's not about sugarcoating anything. It's about having the conversation.

I love C. Northcote Parkinson's quote: "The void created by the failure to communicate is soon filled with poison, drivel, and misrepresentation."

When people are free to talk about not only what didn't work, because a Learning Moment is neither negative nor positive, we talk about Positive Learning Moments. When we talk about Positive Learning Moments, we want to share with people: "Hey, this is what I learned. This is what it did for me. You may want to try that as well."

Here's a Negative Learning Moment: "This is what I've learned and this is what didn't quite go the right way. You may want to look at it a different way." That's what I think is important.

A Learning Moment is not a guilt trip. A Learning Moment is not an opportunity to have a pity party. A Learning Moment is a reality, an outcome. A Learning Moment wasn't exactly the way you thought it was going to be, either in a more positive or a more negative form.

There have been times when people do want to go to a pity party and use the Negative Learning Moment, or the "mistake," as that place to get the security they think a mistake gives them, or "people will come and they'll protect me." They may protect you, but it won't help you because you've got to be able to lift yourself out.

Sometimes we just have to, as leaders, be alongside people and touch their hand and bring them along. I think a lovely leadership vision is someone holding someone's arm, walking along. Not being their crutch, but just holding their arm, helping them get through that little tough time.

We talked a minute ago about belonging. We all know how terrible it feels when we don't think we belong anywhere, when we feel lost, lonely. Think of all those words that are really bad, about bad feelings: lost, lonely, unappreciated, all of that. That's how people feel when they don't belong.

And how do you behave like that? You become run-down, depressed, life hasn't got a meaning. But when you belong—*hey, you are welcome here, hey, you make a difference here, hey, we can help you be better here*—people want to come to work.

We have an employee engagement number in this company of 93%. Ninety-three percent of the people come to work in this company, globally, every day, believing they are doing meaningful work, doing work in the now that benefits them, the company and the community.

Colleen Barrett, president emeritus of Southwest Airlines, shared her perspective on diversity, respect, and trust:

I just don't want people looking at me because, and only because, I'm a woman ... about anything. I want them looking at me for performance, good or bad. I want them to evaluate me that way.

But at the same time, the one criticism I've received from male bosses over the years (not all bosses, I mean, I've been so blessed my best-ever boss and best friend and best mentor has never been this way), but I've had other bosses who would say to me, every time I would get really into a subject, especially if it was more heartfelt than it was strategy-felt, he would say *you're too emotional."*

I would say, "I am not emotional. I am *passionate* about this subject. It has nothing to do with emotions." If I would get upset, he would think, "Oh, that's just the female in her."

That would drive me crazy because I could have some of the loudest disagreements and arguments and pounding on tables with my female friends. *They* never thought I was too emotional. We could be absolutely miles and miles apart on something, but once we discussed it, and we came up with a conclusion—no matter who was the boss and who was the subordinate—we could walk out the door, absolutely fine, as long as I had my say.

Being told I'm too emotional just gets all over me. That just hurts.

> **I have this positive strength; you have that one. If we meld them together, wow, it's pretty darn awesome.**

I can deal with almost anybody and find some way to work with each person. I don't have to adore him or her, as long as I can respect some skill or talent or rank or whatever. I mean, I can be respectful and manage, even if we don't share the same philosophies, because I think having positive differences to offer people is, to me, that's all diversity and inclusion is about.

It doesn't have anything to do with race, color or anything like that. It has to do with "I have this positive strength; you have that one." If we meld them together, wow, it's pretty darn awesome.

I've never dealt with a situation where I couldn't find a way to make a necessary relationship work.

Here's what I don't get. I don't get why those people don't understand their employees, if empowered … they're not going to make any huge changes in terms of a strategy, the frontline … I'm not talking about management but the frontline employees … they can't make huge changes in terms of the financial picture, but they can *own* the solution when it comes to customer loyalty.

Why don't more people see that? All you've got to do is encourage them, embrace them, empower them to do it, and show them the way. You don't have to dictate it.

It doesn't have to be: "Okay. These are the twelve steps you're going to follow." You just have to give them examples, kind of make heroes out of others who are doing it. I mean, we've done that here for forty-three years. We've done it very successfully so people really *own* the brand and the culture.

Colleen went on to share this about the Golden Rule, i.e., doing unto others as you would have them do unto you:

Do you know what the first store name of JC Penney was? *The Golden Rule Store.* That is why I agreed to go on their board.

If Southwest was based on anything, it was based on the Golden Rule. I mean, we talk about it like other people talk about holiday celebrations. It doesn't have to be complicated. There don't have to be eight hundred rules about how you treat people. You just have to practice the Golden Rule, on or off the clock, with each other, with your customers, with anybody you come into contact with. It's really simple.

I'm not saying we never fight with our unions. You know, we're 86% unionized. That's unbelievable. We're so well-known for our good relationships, labor relations or employee relations.

But, if you walk into any other organization, airline or not, it doesn't matter, unionized work force, basically, you walk into a room where there's management and nonmanagement—we don't even think in those terms, really. I mean, we have titles, but they don't mean anything. I've done this when I used to work for law firms. I've walked into union negotiations at other organizations with my lawyer boss. You walk into the room, whether it's big or small, and you know instantly who is management and who is labor. And you can cut the tension with a knife, especially if they're in the middle of negotiations.

At Southwest, you could be in the middle of a ferocious negotiation over something or somebody or some work rule, whatever. But ... if you walk into the room at the beginning of the day, when you walked in as a total stranger you would not know who was who, because they're not on one side versus the other. They're intermingling. They're talking. They know each other by their first names. They know their families. They know something about them because that's who we are.

Do we argue? Yes. But do families argue? Yes. Do we have disagreements? Yes. But there is such a trust there.

Tim Hindes of Stay Metrics shared and expanded on his belief that some of the challenges businesses face are due to an "absence of love."

When we started with two of us in 2008, we basically grew the company to $30 million in under three and a half years. It wasn't the two of us who did it. By the time we were done, we had thirty-five team members. We constantly had people coming into our offices saying, "This guy is talented. He wants to be part of this."

If you dare to create this type of environment, one so unorthodox, you'll find talented people will come to you who don't want to play the old game. So, not only is it the right thing to do, it's a brilliant move.

I do think a lot of the problems we have in business, if you root down to it, are an absence of love and culture at the top.

During my conversation with Britt Berrett of Texas Heath Presbyterian Hospital in Dallas, he asserted this about the importance of trust:

I think it's hard for some folks to get to know their team on a personal level.

I recall one individual who couldn't release the notion she had to be something different than who she was. She couldn't release that notion. So she kept on making missteps. It wasn't until I said, "Listen, I do care about you. I love ya. But you're not going to make wise decisions if you're always looking for how the rest of the team is going to react."

Transformational leaders draw people in by caring about them, caring about what they do, caring about who they are, what their hopes and their aspirations are.

I think what she needed was a sense of trust; a trust that if she made a mistake, that's okay. That's okay because we are going to learn from that.

I moved myself more into a coaching role. We had dialogues time and time again, saying, "You know, I watched you interact with the doctors in this situation. This is what I observed. How'd you think it went?" We had great dialogue.

It wasn't until she allowed a third and a fourth person to enter into that conversation when I knew she trusted us, we were interested in her well-being and the organization's success. Once that happened, magic began.

I work with her today. She's exceptional ... not perfect, nor am I. But I think she trusts us enough, when she makes a mistake, she doesn't have to act the part. She doesn't have to play the game. I think that's exhausting for a lot of people: trying to play the part and act the part.

For me, those relationships are key. Those kinds of relationships, I think, empower success. I really do.

As a leader, that takes humility.

It takes a desire and a hope for the greater good of the organization. It's not about the individual, it's about the collective good of the whole. But, how do you get there?

I think, one, you've got to ask yourself: "How do you draw them in?"

Transformational leaders draw people in by caring about them, caring about what they do, caring about who they are, what their hopes and their aspirations are. Sometimes it's not revealed. Sometimes you've got to dig.

I've got members of my team who have tremendous professional aspirations and I love it. I'm there to help them and support them, to give counsel and guidance. As far as I'm aware, I think they value that. But I do care about them and, I think, because they know I do care for them, they trust me. I would never violate that trust.

When I interviewed Donald Stamets, now general manager of Solage, an Auberge resort in Napa Valley, I asked him, "Before you figured out what worked for you as a heartfelt leader, what kind of mistakes did you experience?"

Donald reflected:

I think as a conference services manager, when you're dealing with a $100,000 piece of business or a million-dollar piece of business, the planner in that company—take Fuji or Colgate— they're giving this power to an individual to make the right decisions, to put them in the right sleeping rooms, to make sure the meeting space is accurate for the meeting they're telling you they need, the power is there, the audio-visual is there, the set-up is correct, the menus, and all that stuff they're giving you that power to do.

In the beginning, before I allowed myself to trust anyone else, I had to do everything myself. So I was working, like, ninety hours a week. But I had total control. I was good. This is my meeting. But I was immature in that position, at that time. As you grow and you learn and you think, "Oh well, let me just give this one thing to Sally and this one thing to Johnny, and this one thing to Alfredo." Oh gosh!

Now, this makes it easier for *me* and you're making *them* happy because you're trusting those individuals to do the work on behalf of the customer, not of me as a conference services manager. I was only the face of the customer. Instead of having the meeting planner talk to the chef, and the set-up guy, and the rooms guy, and the reservations guy, that's what my job was. But pushing off some work to them, to allow them to have that autonomy and that excitement to do the work on behalf of the customer, not Donald, that made them feel good. So that was much easier on me.

Once I learned that, I realized maybe I needed to learn to delegate a little bit more. So, each year as I matured, I learned to delegate. Not that I'm a slacker, pushing off my work on to other people, but trusting them and yet verifying their work. It's also very important to trust, yet verify.

When Dr. Mark asked Howard Behar, former President of Starbucks Coffee, "What does treating people respectfully, nurturing them, look like?" Howard replied this way:

One that comes to mind immediately is this whole concept of trust. You have to give trust before you get it. A lot of leaders say, "Well, I'll give you trust when you prove you're trustworthy." Baloney. You automatically give trust. People must *un-earn* trust.

We need to think with love in our hearts.

The other thing is a word that's not used at all, really, or not much, in the business world: this word called *love*. I'm not talking about the passionate love we have for our spouses or our kids. Not that kind of love. I'm talking about the love and respect we have for human beings. We see value in all human beings. I think we need to think with love in our hearts.

It doesn't mean *don't hold people accountable.* Performance counts in this world, whether it's in a marriage or being a father or mother. It also counts in the business world. We hold people accountable. But it doesn't mean we don't love people who we hold accountable.

I've fired many people, with love in my heart, and they know I cared about them. I told them I cared about them. But we'd had one too many conversations about lack of performance. There were no surprises. Did it always work perfectly? No. But 99% of the time it did.

What that *caring* looks like is, you give trust before you get trust. You give love before you get love. People know the difference. People know when you're just trying to manipulate them. People know when you don't care. You can't hide it.

We hear leaders all the time say, "People are our greatest asset." As soon as I hear that word *asset*, and I've used it before in my own life but I don't anymore, I stiffen up. People are not assets. You *own* assets. "Assets" are trucks and computers and buildings and equipment. And, pretty much, these things always give you what you expect.

People never give each other what they expect. For those of you who are married, I mean, I'm always amazed sometimes at what comes out of my wife's mouth and I've been married for thirty-eight years. You know, you always get unique things because we're human.

So, how does it work, understanding each person as an individual? They're not *assets*. You don't own them. They can choose or not choose to be part of your organization. There's nothing keeping them there, except maybe fear of loss. The more we treat people with caring, with love, the more they want to perform, the more they want to be part of the organization.

Here's how it works in the real world. When you trust people and you give them more responsibility and accountability when they're ready for it—sometimes even when they're not ready for it—the more they want to perform, the more they don't want to let you down. They don't want to let their teammates down. They don't want to let themselves down. It just works. There's no magic here.

I've seen some people, just a few, who are self-destructive, but very few. Most people want to do a good job. You just have to help them get there. That's all. Most of the time it just requires getting out of their way.

Todd Wilcox of the Patriot Defense Group reflected this way about dealing with people who perform at different levels, by nature of where they are in their careers:

> When I'm dealing with people who are new to a task or an industry or an environment, you have to hold their hand. You have to give them more guidance. You might have to micromanage a little bit more. Whereas, if you're working with Special Forces Operators who are older than you are, and have been in the military longer than you have as an officer, you don't have to tell them exactly how to suck eggs. I mean, you have to be pragmatic and you've got to be able to shift back and forth.

Then Todd added:

> Don't allow yourself to be a catalyst for an organization who just says *yes*, who just wants to please. You have to kind of build a culture in which people will speak candidly and know they're not going to get beat up or get fired for speaking truth to those who make the decisions.

I followed up by asking Todd, "Do you think, in your company, people were ever afraid to tell you things?"

> No, I don't think so. We have a pretty flat organization. People speak candidly. Employees understand their input and their opinions on things are valued. They may or may not be taken into account but they're listened to. If not, we always try to justify why we didn't go this way.

When I interviewed Colonel Deb Lewis (US Army, Retired), I commented, "I've heard people say there isn't room for being a heartfelt leader in business. I'm sure there are many who say there is no room for being a heartfelt leader in the military. What would you say to that?"

Colonel Deb responded with this:

All I would suggest is to think about the ways you can make an even greater difference in people's lives. Think not from the head, as "this is what I ought to do," but from the heart, as "what feels right."

By paying attention and listening to others, we soon see the many signs of what's possible that surround us. I think people have the ability, each and every day, to take themselves to another level of caring, unafraid to rely on their *heart* to embrace and get through the tough jobs that need to get done.

> **People have the ability, each and every day, to take themselves to another level of caring, unafraid to rely on their "heart" to embrace and get through the tough jobs that need to get done.**

Soundbite FROM DR. MARK

Authentic = Being emotionally in touch with a story that *serves the higher purpose of inspiring others to do and be more than they thought they could do or be.*

Inauthentic = Being emotionally in touch with selling and motivating others to *serve your personal agenda.*

Being authentic is very important to me because when you're authentic, it makes it easier for people to trust you. When you don't appear authentic, it's tough to come off as heartfelt.

Not betraying the trust of those less powerful than you is one of the best ways to inform yourself about what is the right thing to do. Knowing the right thing—and then doing it—is what causes not just success, but also the peace of mind that comes from a well-lived life.

ACTION STEPS

1 Think about this: Are you interested in those around you?

2 Do they know you care? How do you express your interest in your team members, your boss, your staff, your customers?

3 If someone asked your team members, your boss, your staff, your customers, do you think they would tell others you care about them? What do you think they would say?

SEVEN

Find What Makes Them Tick

I find out what they're good at and,
with what they're good at, how I can motivate
them to make themselves even better.

—DONALD STAMETS
General Manager Flagship Solage, an Auberge Resort

One of the most important factors in motivating and inspiring anyone, be they individual contributors, mid-level managers or executives, is to have a clear understanding of where they are right now. It's also important to check in on a routine basis. Needs and motivations change over time, sometimes by the day.

Some people are motivated by money, but that's certainly not the universal driving force for everyone. You may have learned about Maslow's Hierarchy of Needs in high school, the theory of human motivation. Depending on where an individual is in the scheme of Maslow's needs and social belonging, they may not be excited by the goals or mission of the organization. It's up to leaders to find appropriate ways to align each individual's needs with the needs of the business. It's not that hard to do, but some managers never seem to figure this out.

Understanding my own team members' motivations was one of the most important skills I had to draw from in order to successfully get through that first round of layoffs back at AT&T, when I had to downsize my entire staff. Although that mass layoff was not my idea, I certainly did not want to send those wonderful people away mad. Rather, I wanted to send them off hopeful and inspired that the best part of their life was still ahead. I wanted to help them launch into a new phase of adventure. I have relied heavily upon this gift time and again, both in business and in life.

Anytime I had a particularly difficult situation with a team member, whether they were a direct report, a peer or a boss, I found the best approach was to literally position myself by their side, not behind my desk and certainly not standing over them. Be by their side.

Flash back to my AT&T layoff story in Chapter 3, "When the Going Gets Tough." The day I had to break the news to my team was one of the most difficult days of my career up to that point. Fortunately, my office in the Executive Conference Center was furnished more like a high-priced psychiatrist's office than a typical first-line manager's office, as it included a nice contemporary sofa and dimmable lighting. I used this setting to its fullest effect that day, just as an artistic director on a movie set might.

You may recall from my earlier story how, when my first team member came into my office, I motioned for him to sit on the sofa instead of in one of the chairs on the opposite side of my desk. I immediately came out from behind my desk and sat right next to my team member, turning toward him. I was right there next to this employee as I laid out the details of what the company was going through.

Face reality as it is,

not as it was or as you wish it to be.

—JACK WELCH
Former CEO and Chairman of General Electric

Of course, it was my personal style to already have a pretty clear understanding of where these folks were in their lives. Some were single, some married, one had a young child. We talked about their families, their desires, and personal goals. We talked about what they loved best about their current job and what they felt they'd like to do if they could change anything. We talked about some of the people I could introduce them to in other industries, or what it might be like to start a business, and so on. I committed to help them.

I was by their side at that moment and I was there for them in the days ahead. I sincerely wanted them to be successful. Their success was my success, even if it meant we ultimately would not be working together in this company.

Interestingly, most of us did end up working together again. Two of them started a business together and I hired them back on contract. Others went off to work for some of our customer accounts and we generally won their business when I subsequently went back into sales management. As Paul Spiegelman said, "Never burn a bridge." Instead, focus on building bridges. You'll never regret it.

For better or worse, I got so good at this career redirection process I actually made a habit of helping other managers with the "problem" employees in their own departments. Sometimes I would even offer to transfer the headcount for their "misfits" into my own organization.

With any "problem" employees, I would sit down beside them and brainstorm with them (albeit, with a remote or global team, sometimes I would do this by video conference or phone call). We would explore whatever they thought they might like to do in this organization, along with whatever they did NOT like about their current role. I would try to find out what, if anything, they liked about the jobs they had before. If they could do anything else, what would that be? Where did they hope to be in the future? With me sitting right next to them, sincerely caring about their well-being, they were usually pretty honest with me. What I learned was sometimes rather stunning.

I have long held the belief this is the most important job any manager has to do. As a leader, it was my responsibility to understand what our organization needed to accomplish and then find a way to do it in a way that aligned with each team member's personal motivations and desires.

Sometimes it was easy to fill holes within our current operation by leveraging the strengths new folks brought to the table. Sometimes I would reassign pieces of the work effort between members of the team or in coordination with other departments. Sometimes I would redesign the entire team structure and process flow to better align everyone's personal desires and competencies with the needs of the corporation. Sometimes I would determine an employee was simply not a good fit with this part of the business. Sometimes I could identify other areas of the business where their talents could shine more brightly.

Occasionally, I had to put underperformers on developmental programs. Some I had to manage out of the business. But whenever that happened, very few left dissatisfied. Instead, when people left the firm, the decision was almost always mutual and never a surprise. They generally agreed when the job was not a good match for them. I did my best to help them identify something better outside the organization.

One thing is certain. My teams were almost always ranked at the top when it came to achieving our organizational objectives. My teams were close-knit, even when we worked halfway around the world from each other, because I made a point of spending the time needed to understand what made each one of them tick.

The time spent understanding the motivations of my teams, my peers, my CEOs, or my clients was never time wasted. In fact, it almost always paid dividends. Aside from corporate layoffs that were driven from top down, candid conversations were rarely difficult and never emotional for me. It was just part of doing business. Yet I cared about my coworkers and they felt that in their hearts.

That's what heartfelt leadership is all about. It's not wearing your heart on your sleeve. Heartfelt leadership is reaching out and touching the hearts of others. People who truly believe you care about them will do almost anything for you.

When I was in business development and sales leadership, I always made it a point early in the relationship to ask our customers' decision makers how they were measured from a performance appraisal standpoint. If we knew what their compensation plan was and how they were measured for advancement potential, we could do our best to ensure whatever solution we proposed would help them get ahead. If they trusted we would help them look good, we almost always won the business. Know why clients go to work every day. Know what makes them tick.

Colleen Barrett, president emeritus of Southwest Airlines, worked very closely with Herb Kelleher, cofounder of the company, even before Southwest was created, back when Mr. Kelleher was an attorney in private practice. According to Colleen, she always knew what made him tick and she also made it a point to know what made others tick. During our conversation, Colleen shared this about those early days in Herb Kelleher's law office in San Antonio:

> I've never felt indispensable but I have tried very hard, because over the years, I used to do everything for him. I was his secretary.
>
> As a lawyer, because he didn't ever say "no" to anybody, he would look you straight in the eye and say "I would be happy to do that for you." And he'd mean it, really, from the heart.
>
> You'd say, "Well, when can you have it done?"
>
> He'd say, "What is today?"
>
> You'd say, "Monday."
>
> He'd say, "Well, I can have it done for you by Wednesday."
>
> He wouldn't have a clue Tuesday and Wednesday he wasn't even going to be in the state of Texas. It wasn't as though he was fibbing. He just wasn't aware of what he was doing.
>
> One time I got really upset because I had this lady who called me every day for seven days (he was a general practitioner back then). I said to her, "I'm so sorry, but he's not even in town for three days."

She was crying on the phone. I was just beside myself. So when I went in, I said, "Herb, you told this lady ..."

He looked at me and said, "Her issue is not a big deal. It doesn't really matter if it gets done this month or next month. What I'm working on—" like a murder trial or whatever, "—*this* is important."

I said, "Herb, people don't hire lawyers every day. To her, *this* is the most important thing in her life."

He looked at me. "Well? It's all there; it's just not official."

I said, "No. You don't get it. In her mind *this* is the biggest issue she has ever had in her life. You have to do this."

He'd say, "Well, okay."

So I went in later, after that was over, and I said, "Look. If you under-promise and you over-deliver, you are a hero and people will recommend you to all their friends. You over-promise and under-deliver and you are a scumbag. They will say 'don't call him because he doesn't make good on his commitments.'"

He said, "You know, that's pretty darn right."

The only thing I'm really proud of, I can say I did have an influence, a substantial influence I think, on one philosophy Southwest has had from day one. It was really because I pounded it into Herb when I went to work for him in San Antonio because I'd study human behavior. That's what I do. I just do that: under-promise and over-deliver.

That's really what we've tried to do here.

Paul Spiegelman of the Small Giants Community had this to say about aligning personal values with the values of the business:

I look at this in a business sense because we always talk about mission, vision, values. I'm very focused on that in my company. We talk about the core values we live. But do we talk about the mission, vision, values of the people who work in our businesses? Do we take the time to ask them what's *their* purpose in life? What are *their* core values? How do *they* want to make the world a better place?

Take the time to ask them what's their purpose in life? What are their core values? How do they want to make the world a better place?

I once met a company CEO who said, "Our vision is to enhance the personal, professional, and spiritual lives of our employees." That's it. They were a computer repair shop! Yet they said, "That's just something we do to enable us to enhance the lives of our employees." That's really stuck with me.

If you can show you care and are kind and actually want to help advance someone else's life, that person will fall on a sword for you. As a leader, there's nothing more important.

Whether you're a leader who's ambitious or aspirational, or you're an employee who's coming in and working hard every day, you're doing it for much more than a paycheck. You simply want to feel valued. We all do.

Knowing how difficult it can be to work in an environment where the senior leadership doesn't seem to care about the staff, I asked Britt Berrett, former President of Texas Health Presbyterian Hospital in Dallas, "How do you deal with people who don't necessarily share your values about caring and showing you care?"

Britt said this in response:

That is really a tough one. I think individuals who don't have that sense of caring, it's been programmed into them. In your life experience, in your professional experience, you enter into relationships that are very short in nature. We're not talking about decades, I guess, with very rare exception. These very short periods of time are influenced by their life's experience.

I will admit there are some professions that individuals are driven into because of that sterile environment. Admittedly, finance. They like the detail, the specifics, the objectivity of it all.

My only answer to that is just love them. You just care about them. You prove to them it's okay. It's okay to open yourself up, and when they do open themselves up, you celebrate that. You recognize it and you reward it, both personally and professionally. I think getting to know the team is essential.

In the medical field it's also a huge dilemma because physicians, by their very nature, are scientists. They've been trained to be detailed, unwilling to be personal, and distanced because some of them have to deal with tremendous tragedy. That's been a challenge. Regrettably, there are times when folks just will NOT open themselves up.

You have to decide. Will that lack of trust and caring jeopardize the greater purpose of the organization? If it does, you've got to let them go. As much as you love them, you're true to the mission of the organization. I've had those tough conversations. Some people can get through it and some people can't. When they do, though, it's magical. They cherish that opportunity for the rest of their careers.

> **Genuine leaders ... ask the question, "How do I need to show up to help you?"**

I've had individuals with whom I've worked in the finance area who have realized it is important to care about people. During their professional time together, they see how that's rewarding. Then, when they move on to another opportunity, it's startling. Hopefully they've had enough of an experience in this environment to positively influence their other environments. I hope they do.

I hope the team knows I want to be the best boss they've ever worked for. I ask them point blank. I say, "I want to be the best boss you've ever worked for. What does that look like? And not only to work for but work with. What does that look like?" The descriptions are very diverse.

I had a funny experience with one of our chief officers. I adore her and work very closely with her. For me, my time is very precious. I don't have a lot of slack time; for me, it's my faith, my family, and then my job. I knew there was time we needed to spend together. She needed that one-on-one time. It was in the afternoon, so I said, "Let's go grab lunch."

My favorite lunch restaurant is Wendy's. So, we went off to Wendy's for lunch. I didn't think anything of it. We sat down. I thought we had a good conversation. Later, I found out she was a little put off we went to Wendy's. That message to her was I didn't really care. I didn't really know. She was absolutely right. In the frenzy of the day-to-day, I kind of forgot that. We laugh about it now, but whenever we go out to lunch it's always Wendy's. We've made a joke out of it. But I needed to understand what was important to her and how I needed to show up as a boss.

That's what genuine leaders, I think, do. They ask the question, "How do I need to show up to help you?" You've got to modify your strategy and your behavior to help them grow.

For me, that also is felt, when they know you're putting an effort into it. So, I ask the question, "What can I do to be the best boss you've ever worked with?"

Then I make a point of reminding them. When Boss's Day comes around I say, "Okay, shower me with gifts. This is it. It's time for you to give." If it's a lousy year, then I know I've got to work harder. If it's a good year, I know I have really won the day.

I have a good friend who's an engineer. He just loves doing engineering. He just loves putting things together and he's magnificent. Does he make a lot of money? No. But he's one of the happiest guys I know. He's got a great family. He goes home and doesn't kick the dog. He goes home saying, "You know, I've got some kind of cool stuff, kids! Let me show you this stuff." He does that to me, too. He'll show his stuff to me; it's a blur for me because my mind doesn't work in that way. Those who have not found that passion and that heartfelt leadership, I think they're destined for tragedy.

I think your heartfelt leadership work is illuminating because you're shining a big spotlight on something people are fearful to discuss:

Do I love the work I do?

Is it with purpose and meaning?

Do I love the people with whom I work?

Do I care so much about them I'm willing to invest in them?

When you ask and answer those questions, oooh, that's tough. There are a lot who don't want to go there. But I will tell you, those of us who are there, it feels good. It really does. It's purposeful and meaningful. It's hard and it's exhausting, but guess what, that's life.

I enjoy everyone I work with. I really do. I find them invigorating, different, complex. Sometimes I feel like my role at that senior executive table is like a rodeo, with all these bucking broncos. I'm trying to manage all these strong personalities, to find cohesion and solutions. I think they all play an important role.

Donald Stamets, formerly area managing director for Omni Hotels & Resorts (now with Auberge Resorts), talked to me about the importance of taking an individualized approach:

It's got to be a two-way street. Just make sure the person you're speaking to, or the person you are in a relationship with, you understand his or her needs and wants. You can't do blanket leadership.

Take the 1,100 employees I have. I can't treat them all the same. I have to be able to know Sally from Stephen, from Johnny, from Betty, and provide an individualized approach because everyone is motivated differently. Sometimes people are excited and motivated by money. Sometimes they're competitive. Sometimes it's strong discipline. People are motivated by different things, so an individualized approach is how I've become so successful.

I understand and know people. I have to know their names and their family and what they like to do on the weekends, especially on Amelia Island. It's a very remote location. It's very interesting to me when we're interviewing someone coming in from another city, onto Amelia Island. I ask flat out: "What do you like to do for fun?"

Everyone is like, "This is a business interview. What do you mean, 'what do I like to do for fun?'"

I respond, "It's an island. If you're looking for the best restaurants in the world, and discos, and nightclubs, then you're coming to the wrong place. It's got to be a win for you as much as it is a win for me and the organization."

It's very important for me to get to know those people because it's got to be the right fit in order to be successful, in any location you're in, and specifically here on the island, where we are so far removed and forty-five minutes away from the closest city.

With the individualized approach, I take a look at each of my leaders. I find out what they're good at and, with what they're good at, how I can motivate them to become the best they can be. I focus on an individualized approach.

I know, for example, my general manager Mary. She's extremely good at operations. Anything we do within the resort, operationally focused, I totally back off and let her do it all because that makes her excited. She wants that control.

She's good at it. She loves to delegate and then report back. So I just give that to her.

If I need something done that is a little bit more structured, a little bit more organized, I turn to my director of human resources. Her name is Bonnie Ciballa. She's extremely *chop-chop*. Everything is lined up. She's perfect at that, so I know I can do that to her. I think it's about delegating to their strengths.

You don't learn that early on in your life. I think you probably stub your knees and scrape your nose a little bit by falling down. But once you learn that and you mature enough to understand that you're not losing control, you are actually gaining control by allowing others to do it. That took a while for me to learn.

Garry Ridge of WD-40 shared this story about helping people win at work:

Ken Blanchard is someone who just really believes in the power of the people and getting people engaged. He often says one of the biggest mistakes in a lot of companies is, the only way people know they are doing a good job is someone didn't yell at them today. He's the other side. He's about how you bring out the best in people.

I like Ken because I see a lot of what I want to be in Ken. He's that encouragement, helping people get to the next stage. When we wrote our book together, *Helping People Win at Work*, it's about how we want to help people get an *A*. Taking that fear out is so important.

Ken is about enabling others, encouragement, taking away fear. He's also about justice, and he's also about truth, and he's also about fairness. It's not just all kumbaya. I think one of the greatest learnings I got from Ken is, it's not just about being a nice guy. You've got to be fair. There's got to be equity. There's got to be justice in what you do as well. I really honor Ken for that.

I think the main reason people get out of step with each other is that at the beginning, they haven't confirmed what an *A* looks like. What do you expect from me and what do I expect from you? Can we come to an agreement?

So, the first part of anything is, "Well, let's get to an agreement. What do we want from each other?"

Now we're in a position to be able to help each other get there, instead of arriving at a destination and saying, "You let me down," or "I let you down," because your anticipation of what I was going to deliver, and vice versa, was different. Then we get into a confrontation about "No, you didn't," and "Yes, I did."

If you start off at the beginning, confirming what the outcome is that's going to benefit, or we're both going to agree with, then we both work toward it. So, what does an *A* look like? What do I have to do to help you get that *A*? Or, what does my *A* look like to you and what do you have to do to help me get that *A*? So it's all about identifying the *A*.

Let's use a simple example. One of our values in the company is to create positive, lasting memories. One of the ways we create positive, lasting memories is if a customer calls up to place an order at 8:00 in the morning, someone is going to be there to answer the phone.

Let's say you are working for me in that department. We would agree to that. I would say, "You agree one of our values is to create positive, lasting memories?"

"Yes."

"And to do that you need to be at work at 8:00 in the morning. I think an *A* for us would be you will be here at 8:00 in the morning, right?"

"Okay."

So, time goes on and you come to work late every day. My interaction with you would be, "You come to work late every day. You're not creating a positive, lasting memory. I want to help you get an *A*. What's the problem?"

"I can't wake up in the morning, Garry."

I say, "I tell you what I'm going to do for you. I'm going to buy you an alarm clock. You take that alarm clock and put it beside your bed. Set it for 7:30 and it will go off."

Now you take that alarm clock, but you still come late for work. So I ask, "What's the problem?"

"Well, I did turn the alarm on but when it goes off, I ignore it."

"Humm. I don't think you want to get an *A*. We agreed this was the right outcome."

I could go on and say, "Well, now I'm going to help you even further. I'll call you every morning or I might even come and pick you up at home."

Or, we might come to a conclusion like, "You know what? That *A* doesn't work for me because I'm just not a morning person. I really need to be on the late shift in customer service. Maybe I could transfer to 3:00 in the afternoon."

And guess what? You become an *A* performer because we've identified that's what you're good at. That's just a simplistic way of thinking about it.

On a similar note, Tim Hindes of Stay Metrics shared these two stories with Dr. Mark:

Early on in my career I had a real good example of being in a company where people were engaged. They were rallied around. I saw how fast you could energize people and grow an organization. In that organization, though, I was also able to see through it. It was manipulative.

So, I thought to myself, "What if we took the good from that?"

Meaning, we had people rallying around an organization, but what if you actually started to really take care and consideration for them as a human being, not just as an employee?

Would that work?

By trying to accommodate and respect individuals' needs … people were more engaged in the company. They were more loyal. There was a better spirit of teamwork.

One of the things we did is, we opened up a small office and we practiced all the good we saw from the organization we had left. We didn't take any of the bad, or what we perceived as bad. But we amped it up a little bit, just with small nuances.

"What's my start time?"

"Well, we all need to have start times. What's good for you?"

This was so unorthodox. "What do you mean, 'What's good for me?'"

"Do you need anything specific?"

"Yeah. I've got kids I've got to drop off. I could make it at 8:00."

"Does that stress you?"

"Yeah. It would really be good if I could do an 8:45."

"Well, let's do an 8:45."

We found, just by trying to accommodate and respect individuals' needs, all of a sudden now, people were more engaged in the company. They were more loyal. There was a better spirit of teamwork.

At that time, that was part of a large organization, so there were things structurally we couldn't do, from an HR standpoint. I could not just arbitrarily tell somebody, "Your mother died. You don't have any vacation time, so take the time off and we'll pay you."

But I always thought that was something I would want to do in the next venture.

We were able to start another venture and we amped it up even more. We took all the best practices we had from the last one and we amped it up more.

"When's my lunchtime?"

"Tell you what. Probably eat when you're hungry. Just look around the room and make sure there's enough coverage."

"Hey, we have an emergency crisis in my family."

"Family comes first. Take care of your emergency crisis."

What we found was we were able to really do quite well. We built an organization very, very quickly. Within three years, we were very successful. I attributed that to creating the type of environment people want to be part of.

For me, it's *care and custody*, as I like to think of it. When an employee comes into work and chooses our team, we have *care and custody* of that person and basically their family, almost.

The second thing is the story of my dad, when I was involved in his company. I was a young manager and I'll never forget this. I was a customer service manager and, man, I was *rah-rah!* I was pumped up, fired up. I was in my first management stint.

When orders would come in, these air freight orders, we would work late. It was not uncommon for us to work twelve or fourteen-hour days. I had one employee and I needed my dad's advice as to how to deal with him.

So, I called him up and I said, "Dad, I've got a management issue I need your opinion on."

He said, "Okay. What is it?"

"I've got a guy, and every Wednesday he likes to play volleyball with his wife."

"Okay. Keep talking."

"But Wednesdays, sometimes we'll get a push from a client and it's all hands-on deck. Here we are, 5:30 at night, just getting ready to work another two hours and I hear this guy sheepishly on the phone with his wife saying, 'I know, I'll be leaving in fifteen minutes'. It's frustrating me. It's frustrating my teammates in my department. What do I do?"

He said, "Okay. So, let me get this right. The guy has basically signed up for overtime and he's welching on his commitments for overtime."

"No, no, no. We don't pay overtime."

"You don't pay overtime?"

"No, no. We classify him this way, you know, so we don't have to. I think he's an afternoon supervisor or something, so he's a salaried guy."

"Oh. So, does he know that? Does his start time affect that, because Wednesdays are a different start time?"

"No, no. Start time is 8:00 o'clock."

"So basically, this guy hasn't made a commitment. He's just choosing to spend more time with his family."

"Yeah, yeah."

"What the hell's the matter with you?"

That was my light bulb moment.

Wow. I didn't care about him. I didn't care about his wife. I was so engaged in rallying around this company. Then I looked at my own life. I had neglected my *own* family.

It was probably from that point on I began to understand. No, it doesn't have to be this way.

From that moment on, I think, I saw it really clearly. Not to be critical of business, in general, but I saw it clearly. I started to understand how the game is played and how there is, what I now term, *an absence of love*.

In our company today, we work with a lot of companies that have very high turnover. I think a lot of the problems we have in business are an absence of love.

What is that love? It's care and consideration for the employee.

Some say, "Well, we care. We even have mantras and put up signs like *Customer First.*"

Well, then you're actually saying your employees aren't first.

Dr. Mark interjected, "So you're saying, while customers pay the bills, treat employees like family?"

Yeah, absolutely. When you do this, to a point you made earlier, is it the right thing to do? It's absolutely the right thing to do and it makes wild sense.

Now, granted, we have the same issues anybody else has. We can only pay X amount of wage. But nine out of ten times, in my opinion, it's not wage. It's how they're treated, how they're respected. Do you care about their personal and professional growth? Is that just rhetoric or are you actually coaching them?

When we coach people individually, one of our questions is, "What are your long term goals? It's okay for your long-term goals not to be us."

"What?!"

"I mean, it's okay for it not to be us."

"Well, I always wanted to be a cop."

"Okay, good. How can we help you get there?"

We're not going to fire you and walk you out the door because now you are a disloyal person and you're not going to stay with the company. We want quite the opposite. We want to keep you on the team. You're going to be a great, productive employee. But how can we help you? Perhaps we help you network through our network, or we allow you time to take classes in the evening to reach that goal.

That's the level we've taken it to and to which we want to continue to take it.

I asked Teresa Laraba of Southwest Airlines how she dealt with situations where the employee might not have been a good fit. She advised:

When you hire somebody and you start to realize they're not the kind of person you thought was the right fit for Southwest, the first thing to do is find out why. Sit down with that employee and find out: "Why did you come here? What drew you to Southwest?"

> **One thing missing in so many other companies ... is sitting down with employees and finding out what makes them tick, finding out what drives them, what makes them happy, what they get out of working.**

I think we have a higher purpose, to explain to them what our core values are, to give that employee a chance to determine if they're going to be successful here. I have seen some people leave for all the right reasons and they've been happy to leave because this was not where they wanted to be. I've seen employees who thought because we care, that meant we care no matter how you perform. So, you have to balance that.

I think the one thing missing in so many other companies that Southwest has such a handle on, is sitting down with employees and finding out what makes them tick, finding out what drives them, what makes them happy, what they get out of working at Southwest Airlines. If you determine you're at a crossroads and this isn't the right place for somebody, then they should still have their dignity and move on. Not everybody can be successful here.

You have to enjoy who you work with. You have to be the type of person people enjoy being around, especially in a leadership position. You have to care about what's happening to employees because they're people. They have lives and they can't turn those off when they walk through your doors. So, you have to know about your employees and tap into that.

Todd Wilcox of Patriot Defense Group told his story with a slightly different spin when I commented, "Some folks think of the military man, the Special Forces/CIA tough guy, as very 'command and control.'"

I think that is a stereotype. It's not necessarily so black and white. Even in those organizations that are very macho from the outside, you have to understand how people operate, how they think. You have to inspire them to do things. The best kind of leadership is leadership through admiration. It's not as it would appear from the outside, for those looking into the military, or the CIA, or some of those kinds of paramilitary-type organizations.

Those are very professional people, high-performance individuals. Those individuals are best led when they have a buy-in to what it is you're trying to achieve. So, it's clear communication, open communication, candid communication, where you describe,

"Here's where we want to end up," "Here's the end-state," "This is what we want to achieve," "Let's talk about how we get there best."

Without defining what it is, there's IQ and there's emotional intelligence. Lately, Harvard Business School has been writing a lot about that. They call it EQ. It's the ability to empathize with people.

Colonel Deb Lewis (US Army, Retired) added this interesting perspective:

Appearances can be deceiving and we have to be skilled to look beyond the obvious.

People you see may look successful (again, I say appearances are deceiving), and may appear to have absolutely everything —money, a fabulous career, a loving family. If so, what explains why we're experiencing so many suicides or attacks each year? Too many people are becoming stressed out, focusing on the negative, and disconnecting from life.

Few people are trained or conditioned to anticipate and handle mental hardships in ways that can lead to magical outcomes. When you have the strength to hang in there and keep the faith, it's like facing a difficult divorce, hitting rock-bottom, rising up, and then meeting the person of your dreams. Heartfelt leaders stay in touch and remain steadfast in finding the best ways to make a positive difference in other people's lives, particularly when the going gets tough.

The truth is most people truly *don't care how much you know, until they know how much you care.* That's easy to forget under stress, especially when you're up on a podium or having to speak in front of a large audience. In one-on-one situations or working with people on a day-to-day basis, you rarely worry that others are watching you or about having an impact. Yet, these are exactly the moments, one person at a time, that offer the greatest opportunities to positively impact others over a lifetime. Heartfelt leaders get this.

I mentioned to Colonel Deb that some people say it's not possible to be results-oriented *and* be a heartfelt leader. I asked her to comment on that.

> **We must encourage heartfelt leaders. We must find room in companies for that. The things businesses can measure may not be most important.**

There must be room for heartfelt leaders because we are human beings. We have to live in this world. It's a miracle we even live at all. But the fact is, as human beings, the heart is where we draw our strength from.

How are we able to overcome enormous odds? With *heart*, we're able to understand and push beyond what we think we're capable of. We accomplish the task because we take great care of the people.

When we fail to pay attention to our people—at work, at home, or anywhere else—our experiences and research tell us people are less happy, less successful, and don't feel they're making as much of a difference. Yet, when you choose to hang out with and encourage people who understand the risks and take action anyway, who have that courage to be themselves with people, they will make sure what needs to happen, happens. Businesses which miss or ignore these leaders lose out on this vast potential.

In the meantime, you have plenty of indicators which tell you when people are not working well. The sad news is those indicators are often lagging indicators. They're not immediate and may be tied to people long gone.

I don't know about you, but I'm sure there are people who have been in situations where they were exposed to *toxic people,* who launched into what I call "cockroach attacks" (yelling) or allow "termite invasions" (comments that undermine our efforts). People will leave at the first opportunity. The organization may be making a profit, but they're not sustaining creativity. People avoid talking to each other and sharing ideas. Therefore, you're not effectively utilizing the talents that already exist. It's a very shortsighted way to look at life, as well as business.

We must encourage heartfelt leaders. We must find room in companies for that. The things businesses can measure may not be most important. As Dr. Bill Bellows would tell us, if we want to make sure we are doing what is right, what is best, and better for our future, then we need to pay attention to what matters most and carefully consider our approach to everything.

One day, I just happened to be sitting in an Excellence in Government seminar. A gentleman named Doug Krug was sharing life-changing insights. He began to describe actions designed to bring out the best in everybody. I understood this language fluently and the importance of leaders doing so in our organizations today.

Bringing out the best in us all means everyone is fully engaged. Here, greater talent is available to you as their leader. I bought his book *Enlightened Leadership* and it immediately helped explain why focusing on positivity and what you truly desire, and being a caring, heartfelt leader were so powerful in practice.

Heartfelt leadership is certainly a component of enlightened leadership because enlightened leadership means you understand that larger context of how people make things happen. The heart is where it all begins. It's what Doug Krug would call the *come-from.*

Soundbite FROM DR. MARK

To strengthen your interpersonal influence, don't win arguments. Instead, win hearts and minds.

To invite genuine buy-in and engagement, we need to listen with a strong personal motive to learn and understand. Engage others in their "there."

Understanding a person's hunger and responding to it is one of the most potent tools you will ever discover for getting through to anyone in business or in your personal life.

ACTION STEPS

1 Think about what makes you tick. Ask yourself why you work for the organization you do. Be honest.

2 Realize no one has to work for any specific organization unless, perhaps, you are committed in the military. You alone decide what you do for a living.

3 You can always change your situation. What would you rather be doing?

4 If you have staff reporting to you, have you ever asked them why they work for this organization?

5 Think about how YOU might feel in their shoes. Understand your assessment of how they might feel is not necessarily how they actually do feel. The only way to find out is to ask them. Sit down beside them and ask them. You might be surprised by what you learn.

EIGHT

Live the Vision Together

When you teach the team about the mission, vision, and values, they can be innovative and creative. They can come up with solutions.
—BRITT BERRETT
former President, Texas Health Presbyterian Hospital Dallas

After laying the foundation for a trusting relationship by listening to understand and consistently showing respect for the individual, you can discover common ground together and move on to effectively set meaningful expectations. That's where synergy lies. Explore any objectives team members may have that support your objectives and align them with your organization's vision. This will allow you to head in the same direction in support of the organization's mission.

But when something isn't working out, how do you get on the same page?

Well into my career, I was invited to consider an opportunity with a rapidly growing company known for being heavily male-dominated. About twelve months prior, the CEO/chairman of this company had brought a new president on board, an executive who had spent his entire career up to that point at IBM in the same division I had been associated with several years before. I was informed by the recruiter this new president was looking to change the culture a bit by bringing a strong woman on board into a senior-level role that had never before been held by a woman.

As part of the interview process, I was told I would have to be interviewed by thirteen vice presidents and C-level officers, all men. I would have to receive a thumbs-up from each one in order to qualify for the position. I was intrigued by the opportunity and felt up to the challenge.

It was a long and grueling set of interviews but I believed each interview had gone well and I was still interested in the opportunity when all was said and done.

Ultimately, I was offered the position although I was told there had been one veto, from the chief information officer (CIO). I was perplexed an offer was being extended to me, in light of this particular veto. To the contrary, I learned the president was all the more interested in bringing me on board as a result.

I asked, "Given the significant interaction this position will have with the CIO, isn't the fact he is not in favor of me setting me up for failure?"

The response was something to the effect, "Actions that can't immediately be discussed are in the works. Don't worry about the CIO's veto. You have the full support of all the executives who matter." Assuming this was their way of saying the CIO would not be around long, I accepted the position.

The day I arrived, I found the CIO was still there. But, to my stunned amazement, I was informed the new president had been fired over that weekend. I certainly never expected that to happen. This new state of affairs gave me grave cause for concern, but there I was. So, over the next thirty days I set about making the rounds to get to know my new peers, my staff, and each division head.

I quickly discovered the underpinnings of a major rift among almost all the department heads and the CIO. Yet, as time went on, the CIO remained and the open president's slot was left vacant. At senior staff meetings, my boss would sing my praises to the CEO/chairman. Meanwhile, the CIO seemed to take every opportunity to undermine my credibility. While I had learned long before to hold my own in such cases, this guy was beyond rude.

Finally, one day I had enough of his shenanigans. I entered his office unannounced and gently shut the door behind me.

No matter what message you are about to deliver somewhere, whether it is holding out a hand of friendship, or making clear that you disapprove of something, is the fact that the person sitting across the table is a human being, so the goal is to always establish common ground.

—MADELEINE ALBRIGHT
First female US Secretary of State

I immediately laid my cards on the table. I shared matter-of-factly and unemotionally my impressions of what I had observed during our senior staff meetings. I reminded him it was my responsibility to help his organization, my own organization, and the entire company succeed. It would be difficult for me to help him look good if he was going to take every opportunity to be contentious and condescending toward me in front of our peers and our staffs. He sat there in stone-faced silence. I could see the muscles on the side of his face twitch.

Next, I asked him to share with me what his responsibilities were as CIO. I wanted to understand each of his performance objectives and how his performance was measured so I could be sure to do all I could to help him attain his performance plan. That seemed to catch him off guard. I don't think he had ever been asked that before. Over the next several minutes, I could feel his defensiveness slowly melt away.

Finally, he stood up and walked over to the big floor-to-ceiling whiteboard that covered one of his office walls. He drew multicolored diagrams and flow charts as he laid out his ideas for where he wanted to take the corporate systems architecture.

He was visibly upset as he shared his perception that the various department heads just didn't seem to "get" what he was trying to accomplish. The reality, as I knew it, was several user departments had hired outside technology consultants to design and implement a myriad of disjointed departmental systems which only served to thwart his best efforts.

It finally became clear—he assumed I had been hired to replace him. I was stunned by that, but now I understood why it seemed he had been doing his best to undermine me. I assured him I had not been hired to replace him. In fact, I was quite happy running worldwide business operations and I wanted him to be successful as the CIO. The two of us needed to be a team.

At that point, we each had other meetings to attend. So, we agreed to meet once a week to collaborate on how I and my team might better grease the skids with the various department heads so we could get all of us on the same page and together better enable the company to achieve the objectives laid out by the CEO and the board of directors.

As the weeks went by, the CIO and I were able to get our heads around what was happening in the field and assess why it was happening. Our teams were then able to work more collaboratively with each of the user departments to devise a more streamlined global architecture that would ultimately be more cost-effective for the corporation and yield better business results … a win-win-win for all of us.

It took a while to get there, and it took quite a bit of heartfelt persistence on my part (along with significant coaching for my team, to help them become better team players), but it was really refreshing to finally walk into senior leadership meetings without all the slings and arrows flying. We were finally able to focus on achieving the corporate objectives in unison.

When I spoke to Colleen Barrett at Southwest Airlines about corporate culture and what to do when things aren't working, she had this to say:

We are a very forgiving company if you make a mistake, as long as safety is not involved. We're a very, very forgiving company if somebody takes a little longer.

It's not just words when we say "we hire for attitude and we train for skills." We won't hire a person who *needs,* but doesn't have, the highly skilled technical abilities to perform the job he or she is trying to get, but we turn down highly skilled and talented people every day if something about their attitude turns us off and tells us, not necessarily they're a bad person, but tells us they won't fit within our culture.

Everybody doesn't have to be lovey-dovey. Everybody doesn't have to be touchy-feely.

Everybody doesn't have to be lovey-dovey. Everybody doesn't have to be touchy-feely. I mean, we actually hire *individuals.* We don't hire to fill slots.

Just like parents should, we tell our kids what our expectations are. When I say expectations, they are really requirements. We make it very clear. We don't have 150 rules, but we've got three or four or five which are really, really important. We will hold *ourselves* accountable for them before we hold *you* accountable for them. You've got to do that or you can't lead anything.

We are *not* forgiving about mistakes in attitude and absolutely defined expectations as to what your attitude will be. We just won't forgive.

We actually, years ago, won a lawsuit that the lawyers said, "You cannot win this in court." We said, "Yes, we can." We had fired a flight attendant who never smiled. We showed everything we gave new hires. We showed the expectations we required. We showed, basically: the Golden Rule of behavior, the Warrior Spirit, the Servants Heart, and a Fun-LUVing attitude.

What other company in Corporate America says that's one of the three ingredients you've got to show—a Fun-LUVing attitude? I mean, come on. We want people to be themselves.

We don't want them to be robotic.

And, yes, the judge ruled FOR us and said, "Yes, you can. You can fire for attitude as long as the person was talked to and as long as it was clear the person was given the chance. I'll tell you, that was a happy day for me because I really and truly liked the lawyer we were working with. I was just devastated when he said there was just no way we could win this. But we did.

I used to argue with the people in our People department, which is our HR function. I didn't want to define things.

Even in the *Nuts!* book that Jackie and Kevin Freiberg wrote on Southwest, they came to me and said, "What are your core values?"

I said, "We haven't defined them."

So we gave them total access to our employees, complete, without us there. They could go talk to anybody they wanted to talk to. They did that. And they came back and said, "Well, you've got thirteen core values."

I said, "That's way too many core values."

In the *Nuts!* book they listed *thirteen*. The only argument I had with them was they didn't have the Golden Rule down. I said, "*That's* our #1 core value!"

They said, "That's not a value."

I said, "Oh, yes it is. It is a *value*." We argued about that.

So they did a whole chapter on that. Well, not a chapter but a whole paragraph or two on the Golden Rule. But they still didn't list it.

Well, now we've defined, basically, our leadership expectations. I've got the Golden Rule as big and bold as brass up there on the wall.

I thought if you started defining things, you limit people. If one thing works for Vickie, and another works for me, and a third works for Herb [Kelleher], if it all works together, who cares.

I don't want to define the *Southwest Spirit*. I mean, c'mon … the Southwest Spirit is whatever turns *you* on. You know what I mean?

We came up with what we call "Living the Southwest Way." It's basically three things:

> *Having the Warrior Spirit*
>
> *A Fun-LUVing Attitude*
>
> *And a Servant's Heart.*

That says it all.

Do we talk to our employees about what those mean and how they can be manifested? Yes. But we don't say "you know, smile 24/7," or "You have to say *ma'am* and *sir*." We don't do that because what works for one might not work for another.

Britt Berrett, former president of Texas Health Presbyterian Hospital in Dallas had this to say about team alignment with corporate mission, vision, and values:

When you join an organization, you have to understand what its purpose is, what its meaning is, what it hopes to achieve. What are the aspirations?

Then you ask yourself, "Is the team aligned with that? Do they even know what the goals and the objectives are? Do they even have any idea?"

Most organizations would say, "Yeah, senior management does, but it doesn't trickle down to the staff." That's a problem. That's a problem because in a very dynamic environment the team has to make changes and be nimble in those changes. If they have no idea what the greater goal is, they'll fail to make the right choices. There's analogy after analogy after analogy.

You must align all the employees with the mission, the vision, and the values. It sounds cliché, but it is absolutely true. Why are we here? What do we hope to achieve? What are the guiding principles we're going to live by? If you can articulate that and communicate that through the organization, and not only communicate it but it is felt, then those who don't have alignment, during tough times, they peel off. They disappear. They're obviously not in alignment and easily removed.

That, to me, then allows an organization to be nimbler and move more quickly. But that's a time investment. It's certainly a skill that needs to be revealed and trained on and educated on.

I think some organizations feel like they are, according to your term, *heartfelt*, but they aren't. I think there's great value in helping them reveal where they are. That conversation doesn't occur in the C-suite. That conversation occurs on the floor, with the staff, with the nurse, with the pharmacist, with the technician.

By exploring where you stand as an organization, if everyone understands the mission, vision, and values, then when the white waters of change occur, the organization as a whole can be nimbler and make wiser decisions. Sometimes those decisions emanate from the team.

I think CEOs are smart but they're not that smart. I think the collective intellect of the organization can produce a result that is superior. We know that. We keep on hearing that. The books are written. But it's really tough to get there. I'm reminded of it time and time again, Bill Marriott's favorite reply when he's asked a question is: "I don't know. What do you think?"

As a leader, that takes humility. It takes a desire and a hope for the greater good of the organization. It's not about the individual. It's about the collective good of the whole. But how do you get there?

Curious, I asked Britt, "What would you say to a CEO or executive, maybe not in health care, who has not been getting the kind of results he or she wants? What can that person do?"

He responded:

Good question. I think there are probably two groups.

The ones emerging as leaders, they've got the raw material. Those of us in senior positions, we can see it. But they've got to demonstrate their ability to find success. I watch very carefully potential leaders and how they lead. They're doing all the things we've described.

I grieve over individuals who say, "Oh, I can't do that ... human resources won't let me," or "Oh, I can't do that ... I'm not the boss. When I become the boss, then I'll demonstrate those characteristics. But until that time, uhhh ..."

I grieve for those individuals. My counsel would be: Find a small area, a small team, an accomplishment you can work together to achieve, and do so by bringing the team together. The short-term answers are pretty easy: You do this, you do that, you do this, you do that. The long-term solutions are achieved through building a team.

When I was an assistant administrator, I remember Chuck and me. He was the chief engineer and I was a newly minted assistant administrator. I had food nutritional services, engineering, and housekeeping. Chuck and I spent a lot of time with them asking, "How do we make sure this facility, this hospital, is running like a top?"

Start small. Do small things. Define the team. Identify what the mission, the vision, and the values are of that small team. Create signposts, things to achieve, places to go, things to be recognized. Bring people along with you.

In engineering, this was our responsibility so the clinicians could focus on the clinical care. What do we do?

Chuck said, "You know, I've seen this ..."

We kind of brainstormed and we concluded that success would be achieved by creating sweeps. Each engineer would have a geographic area and they would sweep that area to find all the things that were broken. It was a simple effort. It was a simple process. But, man, was it successful. The only way we were able to do it was by bringing the engineers together to say, "What's our purpose and meaning in life?"

I wasn't the CEO. I wasn't in charge. I wasn't the one from Mount CEO who could dictate. I was an assistant administrator, working with the team to create a solution that was in alignment with the mission, vision, and values. A small effort. A small staff. But people noticed.

It reaffirmed to me the importance of doing that. As my responsibility grew, I used that same type of technique and tool to create that kind of success for a larger organization.

So, to those who are on the road, start small. Do small things. Define the team. Identify what the mission, the vision, and the values are of that small team. Create signposts, things to achieve, places to go, things to be recognized. Bring people along with you. What you'll find is, it's a lot of effort, but boy, is it rewarding. Then, as you achieve success, you'll be given more responsibility.

When you teach the team about the mission, vision, and values, they can be innovative and creative. They can come up with solutions. They can engage a small project test group.

We teach that time and time again. You've got to be able to unleash that potential and encourage. *That* innovation is powerful.

The dilemma you have is, when you do that, you have to accept mistakes. Accept missteps. Be a coach. Be willing to train. It seems a little bizarre for someone in the healthcare world to be speaking of that, right? I mean, it's not well accepted to say "ooops" in the operating room, right? You can't really say, "Ooops, I guess that didn't work."

To which I would respond, "Well, that's true. There are parameters."

All organizations have parameters they need to function. But you can create a lot of creativity and innovation and exploration and not be punitive, but be ever seeking of a learning opportunity. That innovation, then, starts perpetuating. I think that's a neat place to be. Then you draw individuals into your organization when you're innovative.

It's not to say I've always been in innovative organizations. Certainly, some of the things we've described today, my gosh, I'm the least of them to understand these things. But we've seen some success and I'm trying diligently to be humble enough to learn from others and then introduce those possibilities into our organization.

Then, in conclusion, everyone enjoys the success together. You celebrate it. Your accomplishments are more meaningful. Like they say, the colors are richer. When we received *The Best Place to Work* award, I couldn't have been more thrilled. I looked at the team with whom I worked. They had unleashed two thousand employees.

Teaching my corporation that, doing that, unlocks the financials. It unlocks them. Now you have possibilities. That's a great celebration. I've got that picture on my wall at home of us celebrating *The Best Place to Work*. I envision other celebrations we're going to have here at this place in the future. I can vividly imagine it.

Paul Spiegelman looked at it this way:

It's money versus mission. It's people versus profit. Why are we doing what we do?

Inc. magazine, for example, is a publishing company in an industry that's really changing. They are fighting

> **Being mission-driven ... will drive better profits for you. It will make you more money ... caring and treating people well.**

for survival. Their thought is, "If we stick with what we know, can we make more money?" instead of thinking, "Is there something aspirational about what we do? Can we redefine what we do and be more mission-driven?"

Getting over this hump and realizing being mission-driven, in my opinion, will drive better profits for you. It will make you more money. I have felt caring and treating people well was the right thing to do. That's all I know.

So that's how I started a business. I never went to CEO school or leadership school. I just did the best I could. But I also have learned it is good for business. I could be selfish about that and say, "We're in business, not just to help people, but we're in business to make money. We're in business to be profitable. We want to sustain over time." So, selfishly, these kinds of things, I think, are important to know they will drive more profitable business.

Yet, business wasn't wired that way. Leaders lead through command and control, not trust and track. Because of the way the business was built, we have a long way to go to convince people mission drives money. I hope through some of the research that is going to be done over the next few years, we're going to be able to show some of those results.

Then it goes to sitting down, figuring out who we are, and what we are about. You need to get people to click onto something emotionally. You have to find that spot where people go, "Ah ha, I get it! Now tell me and guide me through the process to get there over time."

I'll give an example of what I just did with the company that bought BerylHealth, a $2-billion company with 13,000 employees in twelve countries. The CEO said, "I want to build an employee-focused culture. We're not really employee-focused now. How do we do it?"

I said, "First we have to decide who we are."

What I saw from the outside was a company with four major divisions, all operating completely independently.

I asked the CEO if they had a set of core values. He said, "Well, you've got to give me a while. I've got to go find them."

All the different divisions had different sets of mission statements and visions. So I said, "We have to make a decision. Are we a holding company with a bunch of operating divisions—which is a perfectly reasonable way to run a public company—or are we one company that stands for one thing? Then we can talk about where we go from there."

So, we brought thirty cross-functional leaders together in a room and asked that question. They unanimously told me they wanted to be one company. I said, "Okay. We're going to define our vision."

We defined it in three ways:

First, purpose. How do we make the world a better place?

Second, core values. Which are those behaviors that, no matter what else changes in our business, will never change?

Third, the typical vision or future position that says, "It's five years from now, it's ten years from now. What do we look like at that time?"

We went through that exercise over those couple days.

Now we have that vision. Yet, that vision will not be cemented into our thirteen thousand employees until everyone is living those values every day and making decisions based on that. We have to roll this out in a big way over time.

There's not much more we're going to be doing in the next year than making people realize what they're a part of, what their role is, where we're trying to get, how they're going to help us get there, and what's in it for them if they help us get there.

It's all about the "why we're here" and "why we do our jobs."

Garry Ridge of WD-40 talked to Dr. Mark about leveraging the values of the organization as a protective shield:

One of the ways you do it is to make sure the values in the organization are put around people as a protective shield. Values are the written reminders of the acceptable behaviors in an organization which are there to protect the people within it and enable them to make decisions.

Our #1 value at WD-40 is we value doing the right thing. Now immediately, that puts a protective shield around people because they can freely ask a question: "Is that the right thing to do?"

The #2 value is we value creating positive, lasting memories in all of our relationships. So, if we're in a meeting, or we're in a gathering, or we're in some sort of discussion where there is depressive, aggressive behavior that's uncalled for, instead of saying, "You're acting like a jerk," I can say, "I'm not sure whether that's going to be a really positive, lasting memory when we leave here. Maybe we can approach that a different way."

When you get a set of values that puts this "playground" or this "shield" around people, it says, "I can play here and I can be safe" because they want to be safe.

Then, vision is very important. Our vision is, "To create positive, lasting memories solving problems in factories and the homes of the world." I didn't say, "Our vision is to stop squeaks." We're in the problem-solving business. We want to create memories.

Then people feed us back those memories because our products do astonishing things that make people feel good. They want to belong to WD-40 because they know an interaction with someone is going to be that person telling them how our products made them a hero, and that person's going to feel good about it. Belonging. Memories. It's not rocket science.

Values are the written reminders of the acceptable behaviors in an organization which are there to protect the people within it and enable them to make decisions.

Isn't this just creating a playground around a set of values we would all be able to accept and therefore, we know where it's safe to play? Isn't that what we are doing in an organization? We put a set of values—a fence—around, so now there's a safe place to play? It's really what you would call "aligned values."

Reasonable people who share the same values and absorb the same information will have a very similar outcome or point of view.

Now the three things there: Reasonable. Values. Absorb information. Any time I've been in a conflict or negotiation where it's gone sideways, it's either because one party wasn't reasonable, they didn't share the same values, or one party hadn't absorbed the information. They didn't understand as much as the other party.

I would say, "Okay. We're both reasonable. So, now what do we know? I'll lend you my eyes. You lend me yours and let's see what we both can see," instead of "I know it all and you know nothing."

Or, "I'm here to prove you wrong. I'm gonna getcha."

When Dr. Mark asked Garry, "What do you do when people are unwilling or incapable of absorbing the information or they're closed to dialogue or discussion?" Garry responded:

> Well firstly, there is someone who doesn't listen with the intent of being influenced, number one. You should listen with the intent to be influenced.
>
> Or, number two, they've got an ego that's so big. They just think they know it all.
>
> Or, they're afraid. They are afraid if they admit they don't know, then they will lose their self-esteem.
>
> I learned a long time ago, and it's played such a positive part in my life: I am consciously incompetent.
>
> I love three words so much, "**I. DON'T. KNOW.**" I think they're the most powerful words we can use as leaders, to say, "I don't know. Tell me what you know."
>
> Suddenly these barriers come down. Fear goes away. Conversation happens. Dialogue. Learning. Eventually, we come toward a position we both then say we think we agree on.
>
> I think someone who's a "know-it-all" is losing so much. I love telling people, "I don't know." It's amazing how much I learn. "I don't know. Tell me what you know."
>
> I remember I was sitting in a meeting when I first moved here to the United States. It was actually in a room in this building. Someone was presenting something. I sat there for about fifteen minutes. It was a combination of words they were using that I was unfamiliar with and a subject I was not that comfortable with that got me to a point where I put my hand up and said, "I'm sorry, but I have to tell you, I have really no clue what you are talking about."

The whole room gasped, and then sighed. Guess what? I wasn't the only one who was confused. We backed up. The conversation started again.

I think by the time we finished we had a reasonable understanding of what was going on. But if I hadn't said that, the whole room would have walked out uninformed. We would have all wasted many hours. The person presenting would have thought we knew, and we would have gone on to do things that were uninformed. It was amazing to me people were afraid to do that because they were going to lose face. They all wanted to be the smartest guy in the room.

I want to be the dumbest guy in the room. I want to be the last one to know. Not knowing is not a reflection on your intelligence. It's really an acknowledgment of your curiosity. There's a difference between not knowing, not admitting, and not asking. We should be asking, "Why is that so? Why is that like that?"

I've always been really inquisitive. I find myself, today, questioning myself deeper about things I think I believe. Because I want to make sure I'm not biased in my thinking. You know, we get confirmation bias. I think as leaders we've got to check that all the time.

I love the saying, "Be wary of advice from people who don't have to deal with the consequences."

I'm always challenging: "Why? Why?"

Now, that doesn't mean confrontation, but it means "I just want to know."

I think one of the leadership attributes is, you've got to be very curious. Not necessarily confrontational, but you've got to be curious. You don't have to disagree, but poke at things a little bit. I love that saying, "Can I poke at that a little bit?" It translates a lot better than, "I don't believe what you are saying."

I think maybe we should say, "I know *now*. This is what I know now," because tomorrow, things change. New information comes to the table.

Two people with differing points of view are very healthy. It really means this person knows something different than this person. If we can bring it together, we get a new enhanced point of view. That is going to be richer than the two were on their own, without any doubt.

Todd Wilcox of the Patriot Defense Group says this about culture and building consensus:

Nobody has a monopoly on the best ideas, so collaboratively you come up with a strategy. It's not always possible with the time constraints you have, but when time allows, you want to build consensus and then say, "Okay. This is where we're going."

Culture is a big part of what I think heartfelt leadership comes down to. Can you develop a culture within your organization that allows for that kind of style?

Then you make a decision as a leader, on that strategy and then you implement it. I think that gives people that buy-in.

That might be more of the heartfelt leadership you're talking about. It exists. It exists in the military, certainly at the senior levels. It exists, to some extent, in the CIA as well. It's not as macho as you might think.

Culture is a big part of what I think heartfelt leadership comes down to. Can you develop a culture within your organization that allows for that kind of style? Do you groom and develop the people who work for you in such a way they're going to respond to that kind of leadership style?

There have been several times along the way where we were going to go this way, but somebody didn't agree. We'd give them an opportunity to get on board and if they didn't, well, we're going this way.

Going back to the initial premise for heartfelt leadership, I've got a very collaborative, inclusive approach to developing strategy. So I always seek out the input from everybody around me because I want the best plan in place. But once we decide on the plan, now it comes to implementing. We'll adjust as the environment changes from time to time.

We do a lot of what's called "war-gaming," which is a lesson we learned from the military where we try to think three or four steps ahead. Contingency planning: If we do this, then this is what's likely going to come out of it. What is the course of action we are trying to develop? What are the variables along the way which could impact that? If they do, which way will they push us?

We do all that as we go along. That helps. I do it with my key employees. I do it with finance. I do it with personnel, the operations side. We get the right people in the room. We usually try to develop two or three courses of action so we can do a comparison. Then we have a decision matrix and we put in the key components of success. It's pretty analytical. Then we number each course of action based on those variables, those various aspects of success.

It's a numbers game. A lot of times, it's intuitive. You may not get the number you want but there are reasons why you make the decision you make. You may go a different way. But usually, if you're honest in the system, the numbers will tell you which way to go.

Dr. Mark asked Howard Behar, formerly of Starbucks Coffee: "Based on your personal experience, does caring about people and practicing these values lead to increased profits, less turnover, increased market share, and greater customer satisfaction?"

Howard pondered:

That's a good question. I think the caveat is this: Caring about people doesn't ensure success. Not caring about people doesn't ensure success, either. The question is, who do you want to be? How do you want to live your life? What kind of organization do you want?

I will make a case for successful companies I can point out. I should point out I'm a retailer, so those are the companies I'm most familiar with. Starbucks is certainly one. We treated people with respect and dignity. We had good, open, honest communication. And I would say, by any measure, Starbucks has been successful at all levels. Not only on the financial level, but low turnover, high economic performance, global expansion, all the things we talk about in the business climate.

The ones who lose sight of their greater purpose lose sight of why they're there.

Take a company like Costco, same thing. Nordstrom, same thing. There's been company after company. But the ones who lose sight of their greater purpose lose sight of why they're there. They lose sight of the people. They lose sight of their passion for what they're doing. Slowly but surely it destroys an organization.

While chatting with Teresa Laraba at Southwest Airlines, I shared, "Some leaders say 'It's not my job to get people to want to work here. It's not my job to motivate them. They're either motivated or they're not.' What do you think about that?"

Teresa replied:

That's a very interesting question, one we talk about a lot here. There does have to be a core sense in individuals that motivates them to come to work. They have to want to get up in the morning and want to live their lives.

As a leader, it is your responsibility to make sure the workplace is as engaging as it can be, as welcoming as it can be.

But once they get to your place of employment, especially as a leader, it is your responsibility to make sure the workplace is as engaging as it can be, as welcoming as it can be. Especially in our case, you are living out what people expect at Southwest Airlines: a caring environment.

You have to ask some very difficult questions like, "Are there ideas *you* have we haven't brought forward?"

You have to tap into why the people you touch every day think you're not being successful. Then it has to work its way all the way down. Sometimes companies find it's the smallest thing they could be doing differently. They wouldn't know it unless they work their way all the way to a frontline employee.

A lot of CEOs forget that. They look at just their C-suite. They look at just the people they see every day. They forget who may be the lowest level individual on that org chart that's delivering on that service or that product. It could very well be that person making all the difference for you.

If you have a good product and you are financially stable, but you are not as profitable as you would like to be, then there is probably something happening within your organization where people are disconnected. If you don't find out where that disconnect is, you may not be able to turn that corner, to get the profits you want.

If you are in a company that is not making money and it is a very difficult situation for everybody, you still have to take the same steps. But you also have to realize you are dealing with a different reality. It's hard for people to be excited about a company that isn't making money. Unless they understand how to be part of changing that, then you are going to have a hard time keeping employees motivated and motivating yourself.

Retired US Army Colonel Deb Lewis added her own interesting spin:

I'd say being a heartfelt leader is absolutely part and parcel of being in the military. I would say it's essential everywhere else, too, where people gather and work together.

Some people will say it doesn't have a place, or it's something we don't have the luxury of time to do. You may be able to achieve things in the short-term by not being a heartfelt leader, by enforcing the rules and doing only what you are told ... but for enduring success ... there is no way you're going to attract and keep people in your organization and inspire them to do more than what you can explain to them. It's helping them see and access all their talents and bring that to any new situation they face.

It's helping them see and access all their talents and bring that to any new situation they face.

I think we're seeing, in business today, companies that have been around for years suddenly take a nosedive, depending on how they treat people, how they encourage people, and how they care about people. When they face tough situations, they may rise to the occasion or fall apart. The ones who stay in the game and continue to be successful are the ones who are paying attention to those things and are really heartfelt.

One of the best ways to assess a company is how they treat new employees and anyone in the hiring process. I wrote a chapter *Decisions Built to Last* in the book *Decisive Women*. I described the concept of Infinite-Win, something Deb Boelkes and I coined after looking at what mattered in our own successful organizations. Normally, hiring decisions are considered win-lose propositions: One person "wins" the job, and everyone else loses. What happens when we change the rules to infinite-win?

Here, we look for opportunities for positive impacts and caring actions that will achieve enduring success for everyone. Heartfelt leaders naturally look at situations more holistically and care about the intended and unintended consequences every step of the way.

We have so much need in this country today, in this world today. We sure could use many more heartfelt leaders out there bringing people together ... instead of dividing everybody. We have the power within each of us to accomplish the important things we need to accomplish each and every day.

Soundbite FROM DR. MARK

Open your mind to other ways of thinking. The more you are open to hearing other people's logic, data and ideas, and the more you take an interest in how they see and experience the work they're doing, the more readily they'll listen when it's your turn to talk.

Try getting your whole team together for a no-holds-barred discussion of what you're trying to achieve and ask why they have reservations about how (or whether) they can pull it off.

Ask everyone to bring the issues out into the open so you can work on resolving them. You may already know some of the answers or you may not. But frame it as "I could really use your help with this" and encourage people to suggest solutions as a group. It is very disarming—and you'll probably learn a lot. It's worth a try.

ACTION STEPS

1 Think of a past situation in your workplace where something didn't work out well. What, if anything, did you do to get people on the same page?

2 Knowing what you know now, what might you have done differently to foster a better outcome?

3 Think about a situation going on right now in your workplace where things aren't currently working well. What can you do, starting tomorrow, to get people on the same page? Now go with that. You'll very likely be glad you did.

NINE

Give a Power Thank You

I did better because I didn't want to disappoint this individual ...
I expressed my thanks to him for imparting that.
—TODD WILCOX
Chairman, Patriot Defense Group

I have always been a firm believer one of the best ways to motivate anyone—your family, your friends, your peers, your staff and even your superiors—is to express gratitude. It's amazing what the simple act of saying *thank you* can do to get people aligned and make incredible things happen.

We all like to be appreciated. Job satisfaction surveys have proven time and time again, the power of simply appreciating someone's work can be more important than any other factor in employee engagement. When you, as a manager or teammate, appreciate hard work and you express gratitude when it's due, you will likely have a far greater impact on those around you. The recipients of your appreciation will most likely be inspired to put forth an even greater effort to ensure they will be thanked again.

In conducting the interviews for this book and *The WOW Factor Workplace: How to Create a Best Place to Work Culture,* we heard a number of stories from heartfelt leaders, like Teresa Laraba of Southwest Airlines and Paul Spiegelman of Small Giants Community, who shared how they treasure each and every handwritten note card they have received over the years. As Paul Spiegelman told us, "That note you can get from someone … that says, 'thank you, you've changed my life' … is much more powerful, much more valuable, than any amount of money I could have in the bank."

The uniqueness of a handwritten note—especially in this age of emails, text messages, Facebook posts and tweets—will not go unnoticed. The simple act of sending a special thank-you note to a star performer's manager, spouse, parent, or adult child can have an exponential impact. It can help strengthen the high performer's personal life, especially when his/her partner or other family member may have felt he/she, too, had sacrificed—from family time lost or special holiday events cancelled—as a result of the dedicated effort extended by this hard working relation.

Back when I was running a professional services organization at IBM, our team worked on projects as far away as Alaska. The members of our team who worked on the Alaskan projects were sometimes away from home for lengthy periods and missed out on some important family events. I especially appreciated the dedication of these team members since their decision to work on such projects was voluntary.

When we finally completed the Alaskan project, I hosted a big celebration at my home for the entire team and we included their significant others, too. I mailed formal invitations to their homes so the significant others would receive the invitation directly from me, recognizing the celebratory importance.

On the evening of our gathering, my two sons, then ages 5 and 8, joined me and my husband in warmly greeting guests as they arrived at our door. Our boys proudly escorted each guest to the beverage bar and buffet table. My boys were excited to be included as part of my "work team" and I was happy to serve as a role model to one and all.

Once everyone had arrived and had a chance to meet each other's spouses and partners, I made a casual yet heartfelt speech to all the attendees. I publicly recognized the outstanding contributions and accomplishments of each team member. I included stories acknowledging those who had missed anniversary dinners, kids' soccer matches, or birthday parties. I also paid homage to the contributions and sacrifices made by the family members left at home.

As I circled the room recognizing the efforts of each and every person there, I felt the energy and proud excitement grow. I'm not sure who felt more appreciated—my team members or their significant others. My goal was to ensure everyone felt honored, appreciated, and like an important part of our IBM family. The outcome? We succeeded in building an even stronger team bond.

Now let's consider the flip side. What can you do if you failed to appreciate someone who made a valuable contribution to your career, especially if it took years to realize those actions, over the long-term, changed your life? I'll share one example.

For a while at IBM, I reported to Wayne. Wayne could come off as gruff to some, but I knew him to be a big teddy bear if I approached him the right way. I usually enjoyed reporting to Wayne, but occasionally he could frustrate the heck out of me, especially when he wouldn't buy into some proposal I had for a revolutionary new customer system solution or service offering. On more than one occasion when I presented such an idea to Wayne, his answer would be, "No, I don't think so." Thinking the benefits were obvious, I would respond, "But, Wayne …" Eventually he would end the conversation with a firm "No."

The first time this happened I simply walked out of his office dejected and let the idea drop. But the next time I had an idea I truly believed in and Wayne, as usual, responded with "No," I became more determined to find a better way to go about getting his buy-in.

Finally, it dawned on me. Having spent much of my career up to that point in sales, I should've realized that presenting a proposal to Wayne was no different than presenting a proposal to a multimillion dollar customer. I needed to clearly define what was in it for Wayne, our organization, and our company. I needed to give Wayne 100% assurance I was 100% committed to doing whatever it would take to attain the projected return on investment. I needed to explain how supporting my idea would help Wayne achieve his performance objectives. Wayne needed to be convinced he would look like a superstar for supporting my idea, and so would his boss, and on up the chain. I finally "got it."

The next time I presented a big idea to Wayne, he still didn't say "yes," but he didn't say "no." Instead, he said he would think about it. A day or two later I overheard Wayne in the hallway discussing my idea with his boss. A few days after that, Wayne called me into his office and gave me an assignment to create an official business plan for the executives at corporate headquarters. That was what I wanted to hear.

Eventually my big proposal was agreed to at headquarters. I was assigned to establish and lead the national professional service offering I had proposed. But it wasn't until years later I realized Wayne had taught me a valuable lesson: Never take "No" for an answer to something you truly believe in. He also taught me the importance of tapping into each stakeholder's personal priorities, whether they be customers, my own management, or anyone else in life. If it weren't for Wayne, I may not have published this book.

It may now be years after the fact, but it's not too late to give that big power thank you Wayne deserves:

Thank you, Wayne, for keeping your door open and for supporting my ideas once I finally figured it out. You put your own credibility on the line with your superiors on my behalf and, in your own subtle way, you helped me develop as a better professional. You taught me a lesson I will forever continue to pay forward.

As we express our gratitude,
we must never forget that the highest appreciation
is not to utter words but to live by them.

—JOHN F. KENNEDY
35th President of the United States

When Dr. Mark and I interviewed the heartfelt leaders you have met throughout this book, we asked each of them if they had ever taken the opportunity to thank the folks who made the biggest difference in their careers.

Britt Berrett, former President of Texas Health Presbyterian Hospital Dallas, answered this way:

> Regularly. The one that's older, we haven't seen each other for years. I'll drop off pictures of us when we were younger, write him a note. I think I'm good at that, staying in touch with him and expressing gratitude.
>
> I remember when he had his fortieth birthday and I was many years younger. I had T-shirts put together that said "Ken's Fan Club" and we had a party. It was just a silly little thing. I found those pictures when I was going through some files. I sent them off to Ken and said, "You know what? You are the King. Thanks for all you did." You know, it meant a lot to him. He's since retired and is playing with his grandkids. I think that's an important thing to do.
>
> My other great mentor, we exchange emails because he's going through some life decisions. I'm third-party, objective, and can share with him how I would deal with it. Those relationships aren't top-down. They're side-to-side. There was a day when he was my great mentor and there will come a day when I can give him advice and counsel and we'll function as peers. I think you need that. I think you need to find those men and women who really care about you. What a blessing when you work with them.
>
> My assistant, Frankie, is one of those. She is one of the great mentors in my life. She has skills and a personality I just wish I had. She has a caring heart. She teaches me a lot. There are needs she has I meet, and likewise, there are tremendous needs I have. But she keeps me balanced. Those are relationships to cherish. To that end, yeah, I do express gratitude regularly.

Teresa Laraba of Southwest Airlines responded this way when I commented, "It appears Colleen Barrett has meant a lot to you. Have you ever thanked her?"

Oh, yes, all the time.

It's funny. She loves to give gifts; it's her favorite thing to do. She's quite a gift giver. But giving her anything is difficult because she doesn't want for anything. You can give her anything you want and she'll be appreciative of it, but she's just a giver, not a getter.

I actually had one rare opportunity where I had on a shirt she liked. She doesn't like to shop, so she asked me "Will you get me one?"

I said "Of course I will." It was a silly little thing. So, I bought the shirt and got to give it to her. I put a note on it that said, "No, you do not get to give me anything for this. This is the first time I've had a chance to give you a gift I know you want and you can't do anything about it."

She was gracious as always, but it was fun to give her something I knew she wanted and she would wear. I know every time she puts it on that she thinks about me and that makes me feel good.

While interviewing Todd Wilcox, Chairman of Patriot Defense Group, I asked him: "You mentioned a senior officer who taught you a few things. Did you ever thank that individual?"

Todd replied this way:

Yeah, I did. A battalion commander I had during Desert Storm, Lieutenant Colonel Hank Kennison was very instrumental in imprinting upon me some of that EQ, understanding how people think before you try to lead them.

Hank Kennison went on to be the CEO of a company called Wexford Group, which was bought out by CACI, a big defense contractor. We had come across each other and reconnected. We had a conversation and I expressed to him how much I admired his leadership style.

He was almost that kind of grandfatherly type. At that time I was twenty, or in my twenties, and he was probably in his forties, forty-five or forty eight. So, there was like a generation between us. But he had the kind of grandfatherly leadership style which was harsh when he needed to be, soft when he needed to be. You didn't want to disappoint him.

It had a lasting impact on me because that was the kind of leadership style I was most reactive to. I did better because I didn't want to disappoint this individual. So, yes, I expressed my thanks to him for imparting that.

When I commented to Colonel Deb Lewis (US Army, Retired), "You talked a bit about the people you felt were heartfelt role models in your life: your father, the people you worked with, your husband. The one gentleman who wasn't part of your family, did you ever have a chance to thank him?" Colonel Deb replied:

I would say Scotty, Command Sergeant Major James O. Scott, knew how much I cared about him. He really made a difference in my life. You're able to share that, not always in words, but certainly in how much you appreciate that person. Years later I was given the opportunity to honor him by writing a chapter in the book, *The Mentor That Matters.* I gave the first copy to his surviving wife and children.

Here is how Donald Stamets, now general manager at Auberge Resorts, responded when I asked if there were certain heartfelt leaders he was most grateful for:

My high school marching band director was a big influence on my life. He taught me teamwork, work ethic, dedication, and respect.

My brother was in band, so I had to do it. I was always the little follower there. When younger, he took clarinet lessons, so he could read music and everything. But when it was my turn, in fourth grade, we did not have the money. So I could not go through flute-a-phone lessons or clarinet lessons or whatever instrument I chose because we just didn't have the money. I understood. It was fine. At that point, honestly, I really wasn't that interested in it anyway.

But when I saw my brother be exposed to this group of two hundred people who were coming together and winning awards and having an amazing life outside of what we had in our home, with taking care of a very sick mother and visiting her in mental institutions, and having to call the police because she was out of control, and all those things we went through as kids, I saw the light at the end of the tunnel.

So, I thought, "I need to get in there, but what am I going to do?" I had no idea. I didn't know how to read music. I used to go to practices after school and watch the band. I would scan, "What can I do? What can I do?"

Then I saw the drum line. There was a guy who played cymbals. I said, "I can walk and count. He's only hitting *one and two and three and four.* I can do that!"

So, I tried out for the drum line in my first year and I got it. In my freshman year, I started hanging out with different sections in the marching band and I picked up one of those rifles they used to twirl, and I was pretty good at it. Within two years I became captain of the rifle squad.

Then in my senior year I tried out for drum major—you know, the guy who stands up on the box to direct everyone. At this point I still didn't know how to read music. But I had a loud mouth, I could clap very loud and I had a lot of friends I had

He taught me teamwork, work ethic, dedication, respect.

made in high school ... and I got the job. My senior year I was the drum major. But I still did not know how to read music. The band director knew that, but he took a chance on me.

Following along this line of discussion, I asked Donald if he ever had a coach or mentor in the business world who helped him become the kind of inspiring heartfelt leader he is now. He responded with this:

> Yes. Mark McKenzie was our Westin Bonaventure assistant director of sales at the time. He was amazing, really taking his time to kind of develop, coach and counsel me on how to make a proper phone introduction, what to do when they come in to the hotel, how to do a good site inspection, what to do to follow-up with them. Again, growing up on food stamps, I wasn't really accustomed to thank-you notes and cards and all that.

> There was another leader in that hotel, from the day I started. Her name was Linda Vasquez. To this day she has a big influence on my career, for sure. She eventually coerced me to leave sales and go into her division, which was convention services. She was the director of convention services at the Bonaventure for fifteen years. Everyone in the meetings industry knows Linda Vasquez. She was a huge mentor to me. My last stint at Westin was in convention services.

> When I worked in room service at the Bonaventure, my manager was Nancy Garcia. She was a huge influence on me, as well. Interesting enough, Nancy and I both worked for Linda in convention services in my last year at the Bonaventure. All three of us worked together, so it was quite unique there.

> I then joined Ritz-Carlton for fifteen years. My first ten years with Ritz-Carlton was in convention services, all because of Linda.

I inquired, "Those folks you mentioned, did you ever thank them?"

> Yes, yes. I will tell you, with Linda Vasquez, constantly. We're still Facebook friends up to today. Probably twice a year, when I have an accomplishment or I feel really proud about something the resort has achieved, I'll send her a note to say, "Thank you."

Nancy, unfortunately, passed away about five years ago. I was able to speak about her brilliance at her funeral. To this day, I'm still good friends with her daughter, Ashley, who, of course, was only like six years old back in the day. Now she's a grown woman with her own children.

Then, there's my band director, David Dilks, an amazing individual. I was living in Miami at the time. I had caught wind my high school was going to recognize him for his accomplishments. My high school had only 750 people. Our band was 220 strong and we won every award under the sun the four years we were there. I should say six years because my brother was two years ahead of me and the band won every award then, too.

The high school was planning something to recognize his ability and his leadership as a teacher. I flew up to New Jersey to speak in front of the entire stadium, to give my thanks to Mr. Dilks for giving me and showing me the courage, the respect, the work ethic, the dedication, what it takes; without risk there is no reward; to push yourself to become better.

Never be afraid to stop and fly back to Jersey to thank your band director.

When Dr. Mark interviewed Howard Behar of Starbucks Coffee, Howard summarized everything this way:

Heartfelt leadership is about putting yourself all out, even when maybe you're not going to get anything back ... even when you might not get *anything* back.

But the craziest damn thing about it is, you always do. You always do.

Soundbite FROM DR. MARK

Looking back, did you ever thank the people who influenced you the most?

I have a keen appreciation of leaders and managers who focus on motivating, inspiring, and setting their subordinates up for success and a disdain for those who manage up, focusing almost entirely on what they can do to curry favor with their superiors while treating those below poorly.

I don't think it is wrong to want to please the people above you, especially those who will give you your performance reviews and determine whether you are promoted and get a raise or the reverse. It only makes sense that you shouldn't ignore that. That's not politics, that's common corporate sense.

The issue I have is with those managers and leaders who manage up exclusively and whose approach to their subordinates ranges from taking them for granted, having no idea what they may be going through in their lives beyond their function to downright abuse and even speaking derisively about them behind their backs. That I find heinous, hideous, and repulsive.

It was observing the extent of greed, ego, selfishness and sole preoccupation with serving a personal agenda AND treating those below them so poorly that contributed to my cofounding Heartfelt Leadership and our global online community, whose mission is "Daring to Care," and carrying out that mission by identifying, celebrating, developing, supporting, empowering, impassioning and emboldening heartfelt leaders to change the world for the better.

Did you know giving thanks can make you healthier and happier? One of the reasons for that is you can't be angry and thankful at the same time.

Anger is a reaction to feeling something is missing, something has gone wrong and you are wounded. Anger comes from a need to retaliate or out of fear of something, or someone, attacking/hurting you again (think wounded animal).

Thankfulness comes from a feeling of wholeness; nothing is missing. There is no one you need to retaliate against. In fact, if you are not a dyed-in-the-wool taker, thankfulness crosses over into wanting to show gratitude by giving it to others.

If you are fortunate enough to have had a boss, a mentor, or someone special who inspired you to become the person you are, have you taken the time to express your gratitude? If you haven't already done so, let that special someone know the difference he/she has made in your career. Don't wait any longer. Find that special person from your life, or the person's next of kin if they're deceased, and deliver a power thank you that has three steps:

Step 1: Thank the person specifically for what he/she did for you.

Step 2: Acknowledge the effort this person took to do that for you (say something like: "I know you didn't have to do ..." or "I know you went out of your way to do ...").

Step 3: State the difference it personally made to you. If you do this step right, you should feel the emotion from your gratitude.

For example:

1. I want to thank you for having taken the time to read this book all the way through to the end.

2. I know how many articles, blogs and books you probably read, including some that don't seem all that immediately relevant to you.

3. The fact that you have read this book helps me to feel that we have listened accurately to your concerns, worries, hopes and dreams. Listening well and being of service are very important to me.

ACTION STEPS

1 Acknowledging a job well done will not soon be forgotten. Your peers and your team members may work even harder to accomplish your goals knowing they'll be appreciated for their hard work and devotion. Below are some ways to add impact with a power thank you. Consider other ways as well that might be even more meaningful to that individual.

2 Publicly recognize your team members' accomplishments.

3 Send a team member a thank-you email and copy your boss. Use Twitter, your blog and even Facebook to recognize the person's good job. Recommend the person's work on LinkedIn.

4 Be original. Make your thank you memorable so that its impact will be long lasting.

5 Send a thank-you note to the team member's special someone, such as their boss, spouse, or adult child. Your thank you will have a much bigger impact if you express your appreciation to that special someone who may feel they also sacrificed while your team member was working on your project. Have your boss recognize that team member. That recognition could be in the form of a phone call, an email, or a memo.

6 If the team member reports to someone outside of your organization, have your boss call that person's boss.

7 Be sure to thank your superiors (without going overboard). Let your manager and his/her manager know how much you appreciate their support of you, your team and your project.

8 Always remember the uniqueness and power of a handwritten note.

TEN

A Powerful Example

*Doing what is right, from a heartfelt place,
allows us to 'BE' by example and show that
Heartfelt Leadership has a place.*

—ALISHA TAFF
Girl Friday, The Rock Front Ranch

In the opening chapter of this book, I shared the story of how Dr. Mark and I conducted the world's first Heartfelt Leadership symposium in Southern California. I also mentioned how overwhelmingly positive the audience response was following the conference.

Since Chapter 9, "Give a Power Thank You," was about showing gratitude to those who had a profound impact on your life, it seems appropriate now to share at least one real world example of a power thank you Dr. Mark and I received from an attendee of that very first Heartfelt Leadership symposium. This power thank you letter was, and still is, especially meaningful to both of us. Read on and I'm sure you'll see why:

Dear Mark and Deb,

I want to take the time to thank you both for what you are doing to encourage people to believe in their ability to be heartfelt. I appreciate the effort and time it takes you to continue to inspire people with your insights and experience through the process of trying to do better.

I have had an opportunity to ruminate the last few days since the Heartfelt Leadership conference in Irvine. Here is what struck me:

1. Many of the participants made comments about wanting to change the current negative management culture that they were experiencing. My observation is that we can't change anyone or anything else except ourselves by BE-ing the change we want to SEE.

   Doing what is right, from a heartfelt place, allows us to BE by example and show that heartfelt leadership has a place. When others see the positive end results of conflict resolution in a heartfelt manner, those with awareness can recognize there is a better way and seek it for themselves. It isn't enough to talk about it, but talking about it allows us to reinforce the skills and ideas to have better daily practice when those challenges arise.

2. Many of the participants commented on their inability to be themselves in the workplace. I was fairly overwhelmed by the number of folks who raised their hands when the question arose: "Are you the same person at home as you are at work?" The majority of the room raised their hand to respond: NO. A person forced to be disingenuous to protect their occupation isn't being true to one's self. It might be time for those people to decide if their career choices are moving them forward or holding them back in their heart. Your speakers love their work—their passion has allowed them to do amazing things for others because they CAN be heartfelt—they followed the calling of their heart.

3. Development of heartfelt leadership and male-dominated management. The only way to improve is to expose the tenets of heartfelt leadership to young people. It won't matter if the management is male or female if the leaders are truly heartfelt. Those could be done through pioneering school leadership programs within school government.

There are men currently in management who are willing and able to incorporate heartfelt leadership to balance stockholders and employees. We have a local business on the Central California Coast - Farm Supply Company. Its CEO since 1966, Jim Brabeck, has always been a heartfelt leader, I think before heartfelt was coined. Like your speakers, he is an exceptionally heartfelt man and he directly has contributed to his company becoming exceptional in integrity, employee loyalty and productivity. So, it can be done!

I hope that you will continue your pioneering work to help us all incorporate heartfelt leadership into our lives, on every level. I am so grateful for your efforts.

Thank you,
Alisha Taff
The Rock Front Ranch

Dr. Mark and I now extend our thanks to you, Alisha Taff. Not only did your power thank you touch our hearts, your heartfelt message gave Dr. Mark and me the inspiration and encouragement *we* needed to seek out the Heartfelt Leaders we introduced in this book and convey their valuable insights to a heartfelt-hungry world.

In closing, our heartfelt thanks go to you, dear reader. Your taking this journey with us is the wind beneath our wings. Together we can change the world for the better, one relationship at a time, starting right now.

Now It's Up to You

Thank you for daring to care.

A s I conclude this book, I want to assure you this is not the end or even goodbye. It's but the first step in what can certainly be an extremely rewarding, lifelong leadership development journey. It's now up to you to proudly assume the mantle of Heartfelt Leadership.

Yet, before you go out into the world on this life enriching adventure, let's first revisit the little exercise Dr. Mark led you through in the Foreword of *Heartfelt Leadership*.

Say the term **Heartfelt Leadership** slowly, three times, with deep breaths in between each time you say it.

Heartfelt Leadership

Heartfelt Leadership

Heartfelt Leadership

Now, think seriously about how desperately the world needs fewer heartless leaders and more *heartfelt* leaders.

Say the term Heartfelt Leadership slowly, once more. Now exhale.

You know it is too important to not make happen.

It is up to you to be what the world most needs: a heartfelt leader, starting now.

It is up to you to be that heartfelt leader … for as long as you may lead … whomever, or whatever, and wherever you may lead. Rest assured, Dr. Mark and I believe in you. We know you can do it. You *get it* now.

Take a moment to think back over the course of your life. Identify and describe to yourself the one most heartfelt leader you have ever known. This person may not have been anyone you ever worked for or even worked with. This most heartfelt leader may have been someone you only read about, perhaps in this book, or saw on television or in the movies, perhaps very long ago.

But whoever this heartfelt leader was, think about how this person made you *feel*.

Ask yourself what you could do to modify your behavior such that whenever you deal with anyone at work, or in your community, or wherever you may go, you can make that individual feel that inspired.

Consider now how your career and the results you might achieve in life, going forward, could be even more successful if you were to become an even *more* heartfelt leader. What might be the upside?

Think about what you will do differently, to be that more inspiring heartfelt leader, starting today.

If this notion scares you a little, that's not a bad thing. Anytime you step beyond your comfort zone it can be scary. Yes, that's a good thing ... it means you are envisioning *beyond* where you currently are on your leadership journey.

Continue this *beyond* kind of thinking to that heartfelt leadership kind of place. Continue this practice each and every day.

Dare to care enough to become the kind of heartfelt leader who truly WOWs and inspires everyone around you.

And ... consider sharing this special acknowledgment, and commitment, with your own most-beloved heartfelt leader, even if it's only possible through prayer:

In Recognition of a Heartfelt Leader

Thank you for believing in me when I didn't;

Thank you for standing up for me, when I couldn't;

Thank you for sticking up for me, when I wanted to give up;

Thank you for pushing me to do what I didn't think I could;

Thank you for daring to care.

You have made a difference in my life.

I will pay this forward.

Keep in mind, if you ever need help, or a refresher, or even just some encouragement now and then, we are here for you. Visit us at *HeartfeltLeadership.com*. Read the blogs and the stories—they can be yours! Attend, participate in, or even coordinate a Heartfelt Leadership symposium within your company or professional association. You can connect with me through my website to set up a date.

If you haven't already done so, read the prequel to this book, *The WOW Factor Workplace.* It just might give you whatever extra wind you may need beneath your wings to continue on your journey to becoming an even more inspiring heartfelt leader as time goes by.

I am thrilled to have you with us on this oh-so-important mission.

I am counting on you.

Thank you for daring to care ...

—Deb Boelkes

About the Author

Deb Boelkes founded Business World Rising over a decade ago, with a dedication to accelerate the advancement of high-potential business women, and men, to the top of industry-leading "Best Place to Work" organizations.

During her 30 years' experience building and leading Sales, Marketing and Professional Services organizations within global Fortune 150 technology firms, Deb earned her long-held reputation as a high energy, heartfelt leader who gets things done.

Having ascended her own career ladder within male-dominated corporations, Deb knows only too well the challenges women, in particular, can face in their efforts to achieve career and corporate success. She knows how certain attitudes and behaviors can undermine personal advancement, team performance and interdepartmental cohesion. She also knows the real culprit … and solution … emanates from the heart of leadership.

Deb is as passionate about the messages conveyed in this book as she is about helping organizations and rising stars establish and achieve their own visions of success. In addition to her vibrant focus on public speaking; producing Best Place to Work and Heartfelt Leadership symposiums; and mentoring high-potential heartfelt leaders, Deb continues to enjoy interviewing and learning from other heartfelt leaders across the country and around the world.

She has worked with clients as diverse as Experian, Merrill Lynch, Smashbox Cosmetics, Segerstrom Center for the Arts, Toshiba, and Junior Achievement.

Deb received her Bachelor's degree in Business Administration and her MBA in Management Information Systems from the University of Rhode Island. She lives on Amelia Island in northeast Florida with her husband, Chris. Together, they have three grown sons and three granddaughters.

About Mark Goulston, M.D.

Dr. Mark Goulston, cofounder of Heartfelt Leadership, is a business psychiatrist and the author of seven prior books ... with his book, *Just Listen: Discover the Secret to Getting Through to Absolutely Anyone,* now the top book on listening in the world. As a result, Dr. Mark has become one of world's preeminent experts on empathic listening.

Also the founder of @wmystglobal, Dr. Mark is an executive coach, mentor and confidante to leaders from startups to the Fortune 100. He speaks globally on leadership, communication and influence. He hosts the critically acclaimed podcast, My Wakeup Call, where he interviews influencers about their personal journeys and wakeup calls that led them to where they are now. He is regularly quoted and featured in print, radio, podcast, television including: *Harvard Business Review, Wall Street Journal, Fortune, Forbes, Inc., Fast Company, Business Insider*, CNN, BBC-TV, ABC/NBC/CBS News and he was the focus of a PBS television special on listening.

How to Work with Deb

Deb Boelkes' greatest value lies in inspiring leaders to embody a new kind of leadership style ... one that fosters an inviting and energizing culture and espirit de corps; one that produces and sustains greater employee and customer loyalty; one that consistently delivers a healthy impact on the bottom line ... heartfelt leadership.

Neither heartfelt leadership nor the creation of an engaging Best Place to Work culture can be learned through standard training techniques. Passions must be stirred and inspired. Hearts must be reached. That's what Deb does best.

Deb gives enlightening keynote speeches. She produces eye-opening symposiums, conducts energizing workshops, and consults with executives and high-potential leaders at all levels.

Deb Boelkes and Dr. Mark Goulston, together, orchestrate riveting Heartfelt Leadership symposiums for corporations, universities, government entities, not-for-profit organizations, and professional societies. Consider sponsoring a Best Place to Work or Heartfelt Leadership symposium as a new way to attract and retain the superstar leaders of tomorrow.

There has never been a better time to take your leadership and your organization to a whole new level ... to a Best Place to Work level ... through heartfelt leadership. Contact Deb today.

Deb Boelkes

FOUNDER, BUSINESS WORLD RISING, LLC

Deb.Boelkes@BWRising.com

Office: +1 (904) 310-9602

DebBoelkes.com | BusinessWorldRising.com
HeartfeltLeadership.com

LinkedIn.com/in/debboelkes/

Twitter: @DebBoelkes

Instagram: debboelkes

With Heartfelt Gratitude

This book and its prequel, *The WOW Factor Workplace: How to Create a Best Place to Work Culture,* would never have come to life without the inspiration, support and involvement of so many wonderful people, most especially my husband, Chris.

Chris has been the wind beneath my wings ever since that day I first met him, over 30 years ago, at IBM. He is the love of my life, my very best friend, the most trustworthy business partner anyone could have, and fixer of all things technology related. His calm, cool, gentle, and always ready and willing "of course, I can take care of that for you, dear" approach keeps me balanced and smiling, even in the most frustrating of situations.

From day one, Chris saw a spark in me I didn't see in myself. He has always encouraged me to be my most authentic, heartfelt self, and the very best version of me I could possibly be at work, at home, and in the community. He believes in me with every challenge I undertake. He stands up for me on every, albeit rare, occasion when I can't seem to do so for myself. He inspires me to continue pursuing my dreams, even when it would be far easier on him if I threw in the towel. He happily travels the world with me and even, these days, happily does the laundry.

He lovingly lifts me up when I stumble and then encourages me to try flying instead. He's the smartest, fairest, most honest, and dedicated man I know. He has blessed my life in more ways than I could ever count.

Then there is Dr. Mark Goulston. Without him, neither *The WOW Factor Workplace*, nor *Heartfelt Leadership* would have ever been written. I never even imagined becoming an author before I met Mark. But because I so believed in *him* after reading his book *Just Listen*—which, in my humble opinion, is the best leadership book ever—I agreed to embark on this writing adventure with him when he came up with the idea.

Now that all is said and done, I'll admit Dr. Mark has always scared me just a bit, like a big brother who reads minds. Yet I couldn't be more grateful for the fact that he entered my life almost a decade ago, at that women's leadership conference in Santa Monica where I first met him. I wouldn't trade his friendship, partnership, or mentorship for anything. I miss him more than he knows, now that we no longer live on the same coast.

Now I must recognize, with the highest of praise, the two people on this planet who have had the most profound effect on my life—my mom and dad. These two loving, caring, encouraging mentors, and role models became my mom and dad only by the grace of God—in this case, sixteen years after I was born.

I have thanked the good Lord every single day since that chance meeting with their oldest daughter, Jenny, as I sat outside the counselor's office at Corona del Mar High School to enroll myself in the junior class. I can't imagine what might have become of my life had this wonderful family not taken me in as their own, at that very moment in time. They are all precious jewels to me and each is the personification of Heartfelt Leadership.

On a different note, I really must thank the name unknown gentleman in the audience at that technology association event several years ago when I participated on that executive panel on Passion and Engagement—the man who stood up, pointed at me, and condescendingly announced "You lead from your *heart* ... and we all know there is no room for *that* in business." Honestly, if I hadn't been so downright flabbergasted by his absolutely outrageous and moronic remark, I may have never become so passionately inspired to write either *The WOW Factor Workplace* or this book, *Heartfelt Leadership.* Everything happens for a reason.

I must now take a moment to thank, from the bottom of my heart, each and every one of the Heartfelt Leaders interviewed and highlighted in both of these two books. I learned so much from each one of them. In their own unique ways, each instilled in me a now unshakable belief that what I had always suspected was the best way to lead, *really is* the best way to lead. I'm grateful to now be assured that the best of the very best leaders indeed lead this way. Many thanks to:

Colleen Barrett, President Emeritus, Southwest Airlines. The instant I met Colleen, I felt I had known her forever. She wins the prize in terms of her ability to spend 90 minutes answering just one question, and in the process cover everything anyone might ever want to know about Heartfelt Leadership. Thank you also, Colleen, for introducing me to Herb Kelleher, the handsome and extremely gracious gentleman in the adjoining office, and the cofounder of Southwest Airlines. I've never received such a warm and welcoming hug from any business man in my life than when you introduced me to Herb. I'm sure he is truly missed by thousands.

Howard Behar, the now retired President of Starbucks Coffee. While Dr. Mark had the real pleasure of interviewing Howard, I took great joy in transcribing those interview videos. Howard wins the prize for most authentically bearing the depths of his soul to the world. He was a very brave man to share how he dealt with the depression that cast such a dark shadow over him when he left a career he so loved. I truly hope to meet you in person someday, Howard.

Britt Berrett, now Program Director and faculty member at the University of Texas at Dallas. I could have easily spent the entire day interviewing Britt when he was then President and Executive VP at Texas Health Presbyterian Hospital, Dallas. Britt has a very special way to put almost anyone instantly at ease. I felt honored by his very thoughtful interest in Dr. Mark's and my exploration of and our "shining a spotlight" on the topic of Heartfelt Leadership. Anyone lucky enough to take one of Britt's Healthcare Administration classes at the Jindal School at UT will be lucky indeed to have a professor so grounded in reality, someone with such passion for healthcare administration.

Tim Hindes, CEO of Stay Metrics in South Bend, Indiana. Tim made an incredibly unusual career jump, from truck driver to CEO of a company aimed at keeping truckers happy and "around for the long haul." As with all our Heartfelt Leaders in these two books, Tim is truly genuine and passionate about building and sustaining a Best Place to Work. I can't help but feel his passion through his stories.

Teresa Laraba, then Senior Vice President of Customers for Southwest Airlines, who sadly passed away at her home from cancer on Christmas day, 2015. While I had only requested an interview with Colleen Barrett at Southwest Airlines, I am so grateful that Colleen insisted I take the time to interview Teresa. She was truly the embodiment of Heartfelt Leadership. Teresa eagerly jumped at the chance to tell her story. You would have thought it was the most exciting opportunity she had ever been offered. Anyone who ever met her surely loved her. I have no doubt the angels welcomed her with open arms and heaven is now an even better place, thanks to Teresa. She will forever be lovingly missed.

Colonel Deb Lewis (USA, Retired). The first time I met Col. Deb was when she served as a keynote speaker for our very first Business Women Rising - Leadership Vistas symposium. I was immediately impressed with her. How any woman could successfully complete four years at the US Military Academy at West Point in the first class to allow women plebes is beyond me. This amazing woman is certainly stronger than most. She is tough minded yet humble, heartfelt and positive. Col. Deb quickly became one of my dearest friends. I very much look forward to completing the book we began writing together a few years back, *Infinite Win*.

Rein Preik, CEO Emeritus of Chemcraft International. I have never met a more down to earth, humble, and God loving human being. Anyone who meets him is instantly drawn to him. It's hard to imagine how anyone could survive the poverty and hardships of wartime East Germany under the Hitler regime. As a child, Rein relocated from country to country for months, with little to eat and taking no more than the clothing he wore. Nevertheless, he went on to become a successful and beloved business leader who has always given the credit for his success to his Lord. A day with Rein will make anyone a believer.

Garry Ridge, Chairman and CEO of the WD-40 Company. I was originally scheduled to interview Garry myself. I was so looking forward to interviewing him until my husband was diagnosed with late stage cancer, which turned our lives upside down. Dr. Mark graciously filled in for me to conduct the interview. Nevertheless, Garry has been incredibly supportive and to this day jumps at the chance to dialogue by email. He never fails to add glowing online remarks in praise of our efforts on social media. Garry deserves his #1 rating as a Best Place to Work Heartfelt Leader.

Paul Spiegelman, Cofounder of the Small Giants Community. When Dr. Mark sent me the video of his interview with Paul, I was mesmerized. I watched it over and over. What a wonderfully straight forward, open, thoughtful, and candid heartfelt leader … and a genuinely nice guy. In fact, of all the amazing people we interviewed, Paul is the only one who focused on the importance of being *nice*. His father was *nice*, he always wanted to be known for being *nice*, and he even asks his kids if their teachers are *nice*. Just imagine how much nicer the world would be if everyone was *nice*. Think about it.

Donald Stamets, General Manager, Auberge Resorts Collection. One cannot know Donald and not feel special when with him.

Donald exudes a passion for hospitality … or as he calls it, aggressive hospitality. I have observed Donald in a variety of tough situations over the years, yet he remains the consummate gentleman, keeps a smile on his face, and aims to please. I'd like to think I'm pretty good at those things myself, but I admit he wins, hands down. He's a remarkable hotelier.

Todd Wilcox, founder and Executive Chairman of Patriot Defense Group. The minute I laid eyes on Todd Wilcox, when he was a primary candidate for US Senator for the state of Florida, I immediately knew Todd was special. Very professional, polished, and spoke from the heart. He displayed true patriotism and a love for country. I was disappointed to learn he ultimately withdrew his name when Senator Marco Rubio decided, at the eleventh hour, to run again. I decided then and there to learn more about him as a businessman. He's definitely the kind of American you could trust with your life. I feel blessed and honored to know him.

I'd also like to thank a few more wonderful people at Southwest Airlines: one I had the honor to interview as yet another exemplary heartfelt leader, Ellen Torbert, Vice President of Diversity and Inclusion; Executive Assistant to Colleen Barrett, Vicki Shular, who coordinated calendars and maintained ongoing communications over the long-term; and Senior Vice President & Chief Communications Officer, Linda Rutherford, who oversaw Legal and PR approvals for me to include Colleen's and Teresa's interviews in the book, and proactively wrote a comment in praise for the books. My sincerest appreciation goes to everyone at Southwest Airlines who helped put their special LUV in these books.

Thanks as well to the many incredible people with whom Dr. Mark and I conducted video interviews during our Heartfelt Leadership research process, including Frank Bliss, Owner of Bliss Manufacturing; Allen Brown, COO of Lebermuth; Nancy Carriuolo, President, Rhode Island College; Lee J. Colan, Organizational Psychologist, best-selling author, and Cofounder of The L Group; Dr. David Feinberg, President of UCLA Health; Tony Hutti, CEO and Owner, Executive Forums; Jeff Klein, CEO, Working for Good; Lawrence Koh, CEO, IDP; Doug Levy, CEO, MEplusYOU Agency; Tony Maione, President & CEO of United Way, Rhode Island; Cheryl Merchant, President & CEO, Hope Global; Erick Oberholtzer, Cofounder, Tender Greens; Dr. Larry Senn, Founder & Chairman, Senn Delany; Lt. General Martin Steele, US Marine Corps (Retired); Mike Wall, Acting President and CEO at St. John's Health Center of Santa Monica; and Mike Wargo, COO of Hospice Foundation.

A special heartfelt thanks to each of the role model Heartfelt Leadership interviewees who participated in the inaugural Heartfelt Leadership symposium in Southern California: Pat Burns, Director of Communications and Investor Relations for SocialWhirled; Susan Dost, President and CEO of Sheridan In-Home Health Care; Pete Linnett, Founder and CEO, Life Adjustment Team; Joan Lynch, Cofounder & Owner of WagTree; Graciela Meibar, Vice President of Global Sales Training and Global Diversity for Mattel; and Peter Samuelson, "serial pro-social entrepreneur" and film maker. A big thank you also goes to the dozens who attended that very first Heartfelt Leadership symposium and gave us the kind of overwhelming feedback and encouragement Dr. Mark and I needed to continue pursuing the idea of making Heartfelt Leadership the recognized leadership best-practice.

Thanks also to three very special "early in the game" members and contributors to the Heartfelt Leadership LinkedIn group Dr. Mark and I established way-back-when: Arundoy Bhattacharjee, Darrell Janssen, and Kelly McInroy-Edwards.

Of course, neither *The WOW Factor Workplace* nor *Heartfelt Leadership* would be the first class publications they are ultimately becoming without the tremendous advice and efforts of my book production team: Dr. Judith Briles, Author and book publishing expert, *TheBookShepherd.com;* Barb Wilson, Content Editor, *EditPartner.com;* Rebecca Finkel, Book Designer, F+P Graphic Design, *FPGD.com;* John, indexer extraordinaire; and the entire production team at Color House Graphics, with special recognition to Sandy Gould, Direct Sales Manager; Alisha Landheer, Senior Administrative Assistant; and Robert Tissot, Project Manager.

Special thanks also go to my adorable PEO sister, Hillary Rothie, who inspired the overall look and feel of the book covers, designed especially to appeal to a millennial readership.

Thanks, too, to each of the members of Dr. Judith Briles' Friday morning AuthorYOU conference calls. I won't embarrass them by naming names, but they know who they are. I love them all for so generously sharing their writing and marketing hopes, dreams, challenges, ideas, and encouragement.

Looking back now over the course of my leadership life, I'd like to acknowledge my very first professional mentors and friends at AT&T Information Systems: Keith Franks, Stephanie Harwood Doda, and Frank Howley. And a special recognition to my bosses and senior leaders along the way, those I didn't highlight by name in the books, yet ones I have loved, appreciated and learned so much from throughout my career, including Marty Adler, Tony Corollo, Pat Cathey, Doug Coulter, Darr Greenhalgh, Steve Kaufman, Melodie Mayberry-Stewart, Bill Mitchell, Bob Nussbaum, Dick Ranes, Jim Ransco, and Tony Shenuski.

And finally, while I highlighted her in Chapter 1 of *The WOW Factor Workplace*, I'd like to give a special thanks, in praise and honor of the memory of one of my favorite managers, dearest professional friend, and wonderful role model for many women leaders, Cathy Whitaker. I'll see you in heaven, girlfriend.

Index

Other books in the series

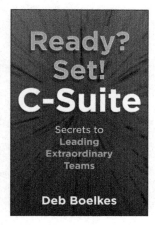

Made in the USA
Monee, IL
12 June 2020